ABI GEZUNT! 2

More CLASSIC JOKES FROM THE JEWISH PRESS

Two Lights
PUBLISHING

ABI GEZUNT! 2

WRITTEN BY ARNOLD FINE

COMPILED BY ZALMAN GOLDSTEIN

DEDICATED TO

Avraham (Arnold) Fine

beloved columnist and senior editor
at The Jewish Press

ABI GEZUNT! 2
MORE CLASSIC JOKES FROM THE JEWISH PRESS

WRITTEN BY Arnold Fine
COMPILED BY Zalman Goldstein

FIRST PRINTING

Reprinted with permission from
The Jewish Press and the Klass family

Copyright ©2019 Zalman Goldstein

An imprint of
The Jewish Learning Group, Inc.
Tel. 1-888-565-3276
www.JewishLearningGroup.com

Comments, Information and Orders
Info@AbiGezuntJokes.com

ISBN-13: 978-1-891293-03-0

Table of Laughs

Introduction

Everyone who knew Arnold Fine describes him as a kind, wise, and warm-hearted person. Those who worked with him for decades describe Arnie, as he was affectionately called, as super talented and enormously dedicated to his work. Above all, his keen sense of humor was the one thing about which everyone raves.

Born in The Bronx in 1924, Fine grew up experiencing the sights, sounds, and smells of New York City in the 1930's and 1940's, which contributed greatly to his later writings. After joining the Navy at the end of WW2, and, a few weeks later, finding himself drafted into the Army, he had the distinction of serving in both the Navy and the Army.

Following the war, Fine worked as a press photographer for several newspapers. Earning his bachelor's degree via the GI bill, and, later on, adding a Masters in Education, led him to become a celebrated Special-Ed teacher in the New York

City school system, and over his career, a pioneer in teaching children with special needs.

In the late 1950's, while shopping his photography services to local newspapers, he met **Rabbi Shalom Klass**, then publisher of the **Brooklyn Weekly** and the one who would later go on to found **The Jewish Press**. The rest, as they say, is history.

Fine's warm and friendly writing style, which spoke to generations of readers both Jewish and non-Jewish alike, helped usher the fledgling **Jewish Press** weekly to one of the top Jewish newspapers in America.

A music lover, who also played clarinet, saxophone, and piano, Fine's creativity never seemed to end. He would teach in the morning and work at **The Jewish Press** for the rest of the day. He started out with writing the paper's front-page stories and other news articles, and, given his knack for words and human emotions, quickly expanded into other editorial functions.

Avraham (Arnold) Fine
(1924-2014)

Commanding a formidable grasp of the English language, he was soon promoted to editor of the paper, eventually rising to become senior editor, a post he proudly and successfully held for decades.

In addition to his serious journalistic writings, Fine's humorous nature found expression in several delightful and light-hearted serial columns which he lovingly tended and nurtured throughout the years. These included the well-loved *Silly World of Chelm*, which was recently gathered and published in a book of the same title, and *I Remember When!*, a highly-entertaining and superbly written column recalling his early memories of growing up in New York City.

And, finally, everyone's favorite joke-of-the-week column tenaciously appearing on the bottom corner of the last page under the heading, *Abi Gezunt!* (Yiddish for, "At least we are healthy!").

Generous by nature, Fine would not let a week go by without sharing with his loyal readers a funny joke or story that he either heard or made up. The funny yarns and witticisms he dispensed in *Abi Gezunt!* were the first stop for many before moving on to tackle that week's world-shaking headlines.

Fine retired at the age of eighty, after more than fifty years of dedicated service at *The Jewish Press*. He later developed Parkinson's disease and, several years later, in 2014, passed away in his sleep. He was buried at the New Montefiore Jewish Cemetery in West Babylon, New York.

Fine was predeceased by his wife in 2006, and is survived by three children, many grandchildren, and great-grandchildren. May his good name and good memory be a blessing!

☆☆

A natural follow up to our recently published book, *"The Silly World of Chelm"* — which gathered more than 150 Chelm tales from the pages of *The Jewish Press* — was bringing together nearly half-a-century of

INTRODUCTION

"Abi Gezunt!" material for everyone's continued delight. The results, following months of laborious yet very enjoyable effort, span two charming volumes.

Volume one contains material relating to *City Life, Jewish Wit, Politics and High Office, Israel, Doctors and Medicine, Old Age, Relationships* and *Little Gems.*

This volume wraps up with *Money and Business, Law and Order, Food and Dining, Parenting and Children, Education, The Pulpit* and *Travel.*

Eternal thanks to *Arnold Fine,* for making us laugh so often and for training us to see and enjoy the lighter side of life.

Tremendous thanks to *Naomi Mauer* and the entire *Klass Family,* for permitting me, once again, to mine, edit, and reprint everyone's beloved material from *The Jewish Press.*

And, once more, huge thanks to *Jerry Greenwald* and *Chumi Friedman,* for their ready assistance with navigating the mountainous archives of *The Jewish Press.*

Last, but not least, special thanks to *Heshy Kornblit,* for getting the ball rolling, *Ginny Westcott* and *Aryeh Friedman* for creative input, *Hershel Rosenbluh* and *my children* for proofreading, and *Suzanne Brandt* and the entire team at *Feldheim* for helping us develop a worldwide readership.

Abi Gezunt!

Zalman Goldstein
Zalman@ZalmanGoldstein.com

Money
& Business

. . . .

A bagel baker I know had to declare bankruptcy recently. He wanted to cheat his customers by making larger holes, but never realized it took more dough to go around the hole!

. . . .

A big business tycoon is breathing his last as his business partner is sitting at his side holding his hand. The tycoon turns to his partner and says, "Sam, I know my end is near, so I want to clear my conscience. I was the one who stole the thousands of dollars that has been missing from our safe over the years. I'm also the one who took our new dress designs and sold them to our competition, even before we produced one dress."

The partner, still holding the dying man's hand, sighed, "That's okay, Myron, I understand. That's why I'm the one who poisoned you!"

. . . .

A big business tycoon always managed to avoid one particular salesman. The guy always got in his hair. Finally, as it must come to all men, the tycoon went to his eternal resting place. When he arrived at the other world, he was met at the gate by the very same salesman he avoided on earth.

"Well, Sam, here I am, ready for that appointment and your order!"

The tycoon snarled back, "What are you talking? I didn't make an appointment with you."

"Don't you remember," clucked the salesman. "Every time I went to your office you'd tell me you'd see me here. Well, here I am!"

. . . .

A bookkeeper goes into her boss's office and says, "Well, we just got a big order from Jones and Company. That order finally puts you in the black."

The boss says, "That's wonderful! Now we can throw out that bottle of red ink and get a fresh bottle of black."

The bookkeeper sighs, "I can't do that. If I bought a bottle of black ink, we'd be in the red again!"

. . . .

A businessman was interviewing applicants for the position of Divisional Manager. He devised a simple test to select the most suitable person for the job. He asked each applicant the question, "What is two and two?"

The first applicant was a journalist. His answer was "twenty-two." The second applicant was an engineer. He pulled out a calculator and showed the answer to be "between 3.999 and 4.001."

The next person was a lawyer. He stated that, "In the case of Jenkins v. Commissioner of Stamp Duties (Qld), two and two was proven to be four."

The last applicant was an accountant. The businessman asked him, "How much is two and two?"

The accountant got up from his chair, went over to the door, closed it, then came back and sat down. He leaned across the desk and said in a low voice, "How much do you want it to be?"

He got the job!

. . . .

A Chinese businessman came to America to see the new type of sewing machine that had been developed. As he was being shown through the ultra-modern plant, the lunchtime chime rang and all the employees shut off their machines and scurried away for their lunch break.

"Look! Look!" he shouted, "They are all escaping! Your employees are escaping! That's what you get for not putting up a big wire fence around them. Foolish Americans!"

The American businessman smiled and said, "Don't worry, they'll be back as soon as I ring the chime again."

The Chinese man was very skeptical.

But then, as the hour passed, the American businessman sounded the chime again, and the employees came scurrying back to their little tables.

"Amazing!" exclaimed the man from China.

"Well," the businessman began, "Now, tell me, how many of our sewing machines are you interested in buying?"

"Sewing machines, nothing," exclaimed the Chinese man, "How much do you want for that chime?"

. . . .

A dress manufacturer from the Garment Center ordered material from a textile firm. A week later, he got a letter from the textile company. The letter read, "We regret we cannot ship your order until full payment has been made on your last order!"

The dress manufacturer sent a reply. It read, "Please cancel my new order. I can't wait that long!"

A dress shop was running a sale. There were customers all over the place, and the sales help were running back and forth. As he recorded an impatient customer's address for a delivery, he sighed warmly, "It's a madhouse — isn't it?"

The woman raised her eyebrows and snapped, "Not at all! It's my private residence!"

. . . .

A famous antique collector, looking for antiques, was passing through a rural community in the Midwest and suddenly noticed a mangy old cat in a store window of an antique book shop. The collector did a double take when he realized that the saucer the cat was sipping the milk from was actually a rare antique worth thousands of dollars. He walked into the store quite casually and told the storeowner that he wanted to buy the cat and offered him $2.

The storeowner said, "I'm sorry but the cat is not for sale!"

The antique collector said, "Look, I need a hungry old tomcat around my house to catch the mice. I'll give you $10!"

The storeowner said, "Sold!"

The antique collector said, "Oh, by the way, I was wondering if you could include that old grungy-looking saucer the cat is eating out of. He seems used to it. It'll save me the trouble of getting him another dish."

The storeowner thought for a moment, then said, "Sorry, Sir. That's my lucky saucer. You see, so far this week I've sold sixty-eight cats!"

A father was trying to teach his son the dress business. "First of all, you must understand business ethics — it is so important! For example, let's say a customer walks in and makes a purchase. She hands you a $10 bill. After she leaves, you discover that there were two $10's stuck together. Here is where business ethics comes in — should you tell your partner or not?"

. . . .

A fellow begged a friend to loan him $100. "I'll pay it back to you the minute I return from Chicago!" the friend declared.

"Okay," the first fellow exclaimed, "But tell me, when exactly are you going to return from Chicago?"

The borrower shrugged, "Who's going?"

. . . .

A fellow on the way to work each day passed a blind man selling pencils. He always put a dime in the old timer's hat, but never took a pencil. Once, he hadn't gone ten feet when the old timer called out, "Mister, pencils are now fifteen cents!"

. . . .

A fellow walked into a men's specialty shop on the Lower East Side and told the salesman what he wanted. The salesman listened intently, then asked, "And what are your hobbies and your educational background and your business?" He then continued to ask about his family and how many boys and how many girls there were. He asked about his political affiliations and even about his wife's ancestry.

"Hey, wait a minute," the irate customer snapped. "I came here to order a suit. Why all these personal questions?"

"Why?" replied the salesman, "Sir, when you are ordering a suit from our establishment, we want the suit to fit the man! The suit will be you! It will not only fit your personality, but your station in life. I want you to know we send away to Australia for just the proper blend of wool. We contact our office in Ireland for the proper material to be used in the lining. We contact our agents in Scotland to obtain the latest in button design. We wire our agents in Israel for just the proper design and style to fit you best.

"Then, when all these things are obtained, we contact our special tailors to come in and cut the garment and then sew it together flawlessly. Then, when you come in for a fitting, we fit it to your frame so that it looks as if it were modeled especially for you!"

"Oh, my goodness!" the customer exclaimed, "I didn't realize you went to all that trouble just to make a suit! You see, I needed the suit for tomorrow — it's for my wedding!"

"Don't worry," reassured the salesman, "You'll have it first thing tomorrow morning!"

A friend recently wrote in to tell me how he wound up in the hospital. "My partner got his Medicare card, and all I said was he should use it in good health!"

. . . .

A Garment Center manufacturer gathered his staff together and announced that his son-in-law was joining the company. "My friends, he is to have no special privileges and you are to treat him just like anyone else who is due to take over the business in a year or two."

. . . .

A Garment Center manufacturer got a call from his supplier. "Hello, Silverman? Listen, when are you going to pay me for those linings?"

Silverman snapped back angrily, "How should I know? I'm a dress manufacturer, not a fortune-teller!"

. . . .

A grocery store in Brooklyn was more than a little annoyed when another one opened up down the block. To remind the public of his reliability, the owner of the store hung out a sign that read, "Established for 25 years!"

The owner of the new grocery store also hung out a sign. It read, "Just established — all fresh food!"

A guest at a very swanky hotel checked out without paying his bill. In true business fashion, the manager of the hotel sent a letter to his customer. It read, "Dear Mr. Goldberg, please send me the amount of your hotel bill and oblige." Goldberg wrote back, "The amount of my bill was $167.50. Yours truly, Hyman Goldberg."

. . . .

A Jewish restaurant owner ran his place of business on the Lower East Side. Set in his ways, the old timer kept his whole bookkeeping system in cigar boxes. He had one box that he kept on his left, in which were his accounts payable. In another cigar box on his right, he kept his receipts.

When his youngest son graduated and obtained his Certified Public Accountant's license, he sat down with his father and questioned, "Dad, I don't understand how you can run a business this way. How do you know what your profits are?"

The old man sat down and explained, "My dear son, when I got off the boat from Poland, some forty years ago, I had nothing but the clothing I was wearing. But, today, thank G-d, your brother is a doctor, you are an accountant, and your sister is a schoolteacher. Your mother and I have a nice car, a house in the city and even a summer home on the lake. We have a steady business, and everything is paid for. So, in answer to your question, add all that together, subtract the clothing I wore when I came to America, and *shoen* — that's the profit!"

A lawyer, who had just lost a $100,000 case for his insurance company, was convinced the man who won was faking an injury to his back. Indignant over the loss, he stepped up to the injured man and said, "You may have cost my company $100,000, but I'm making it my personal business to follow you wherever you go from this day on. And one day, I'm going to catch you in your faking act!"

The man shrugged his shoulders and snapped back, "Listen, you'll never be able to prove a thing, because when I leave this court room, I'm taking an airplane trip to London, England to visit a specialist over there. Maybe he can cure my legs. And if he fails, I'm gonna take a trip to Paris, France with my family to visit a very big specialist over there. And if he can't cure my legs, I'm gonna take a trip to Italy to visit a big leg man over there, and if he can't cure my injury, I'm gonna take an airplane to Israel and visit the Western Wall and pray, and then, boy are you going to see a miracle!'"

. . . .

A local businessman, who was being honored at a dinner, seemed angry. A friend went over to him and said, "Why are you angry? They praised you to the sky. They talked about your charity, your brilliant business sense, and what an extraordinary executive you are. Why are you angry?"

The businessman replied, "Sure! But no one mentioned my humility!"

A local businessman was asked to make a donation to a shul. The businessman apologized and said, "I'm sorry, not this year. Why, last week I lost $500. The week before, $800. And the week before that, $700."

The friend asked, "So why do you stay in business?"

The businessman explained, "Listen, a person has to make a living. Besides, I do a terrific volume!"

. . . .

A local department store announced the sale of the year. Thousands gathered in front of the store even before it opened. Finally, the doors were opened and there was a mad rush. A man who was holding a shopping list from his wife accidentally dropped it and began scurrying around on the floor looking for it.

After some time, he found a piece of paper that resembled his shopping list. As he straightened it out and read the paper, he discovered it was not the shopping list but a printed memo from the store's executive office, which they had printed up in big red letters and distributed to each department head. It read, "Remember, sell last year's merchandise first!"

. . . .

A man purchased a ticket to a show. After the first act, he noticed a vacant seat closer to the stage. As he approached the seat, he asked the person sitting next to the empty seat if it was taken.

"This is my partner's seat," the man explained.

"So, where is your partner?" the man asked.

"He passed away, but I still had the ticket," the person exclaimed.

"Then why didn't you give the ticket to a relative or friend?" the man asked.

"I couldn't," the man explained, "They all went to his funeral."

. . . .

A man walked into Lieberman & Rind, on Stanton Street, and picked out a tie. The clerk wrapped it up and handed it to the man.

"I changed my mind," the customer said, "I think I'd rather take this pair of socks instead."

"Okay," exclaimed the clerk, who took the socks and began to wrap them up. He handed them to the customer who started to walk out of the store.

"Hey, wait a minute," the clerk shouted, "You didn't pay for that!"

The customer turned, slightly hurt, "What are you talking about? I just traded the tie for the socks!"

"Yes," exclaimed the clerk, "But you didn't pay for the tie."

"Of course," exclaimed the customer, "Did I keep it?"

A newcomer to this country was taken to a bank for a loan to go into business with a friend. "Shloimy," exclaimed the newcomer, "I don't understand how this works."

Shloimy explained, "Look at it this way, if you live for five years, you pay back the loan with interest and that's the bank's good luck. But if you should die before the five years, that's *your* good luck!"

· ·

A panhandler stopped a businessman for a handout. "Listen, why don't you learn a skill or study for a profession?" commented the businessman. The panhandler spoke softly, "Listen, I did have a profession. Actually, I'm a writer, and I once even wrote a book, maybe you read it? It was called, "100 Ways to Earn Money."

"So why are you begging?" queried the businessman.

"Why?" responded the beggar, "Because this is one of the ways!"

· ·

A sweet little old lady had lost a large sum of money in the stock market. A neighbor had talked her into buying that particular stock. When she told her son, who was also in the stock market, he asked, "Ma, why didn't you ask me about that stock first?"

The little old lady lowered her eyes and replied softly, "I was afraid you'd tell me not to buy it!"

A young man walked into a clothing store on the Lower East Side and said he wanted to buy a suit. He pointed to a blue serge suit and asked the owner how much he wanted.

"My friend, are you lucky!" exclaimed the storeowner. "You, by a chance of fate, have picked out the very best suit in the house! That suit is a gem! I like to do business with a man who has good taste. And because of that, I'm going to make you a special proposition on that suit. I wouldn't ask you for the $100 the suit costs me. In fact, I wouldn't even ask you $65 — like what I gave it to my son-in-law for. And I wouldn't even ask you $45 — like what I charged my wife's brother. For you, I'm giving the suit away for $35!"

The young man scratched his head, felt the fabric, then said. "Listen, I haven't the heart to give you $35, for this suit. In fact, I wouldn't give you $25. My best offer is $15."

"SOLD!" shouted the merchant, placing it in a box. "That's the way I like to do business! No bargaining! Please come again!"

· ·

A young man walked into a supermarket and approached the manager. "Excuse me sir, do you need a good check-out clerk?" The manager, who was very busy and clearly didn't want to be disturbed, snapped, "No!"

The youth then asked, "Could you use a good stock clerk?"

The manager fumed and shouted, "Nope! I have all the help I need."

The youth smiled and said, "That's great, let me introduce

myself, I'm Morris Goldberg from the Speedy Sign company. Since you need no help, you obviously need to purchase this..." And he handed him a "NO HELP WANTED" sign.

• •

A young salesman walked out of his boss's office and said to a person waiting to go in. "You know that old codger is the meanest guy I've ever met."

The person smiled and said, "Do you know who I am? I'm the boss's son."

The young man paled and asked, "And do you know who I am?"

"No," replied the son.

"Thank G-d!" gasped the young man, as he ran out the door.

• •

A be and Sam had been partners for many years. One day, Abe told his friend that he was going to take a trip to Europe and handed him a key.

"My good friend," exclaimed Abe, "This is the key to my personal safe in my office. There, I have all my important papers and over $100,000 in cash in small bills that I have put away over the years. If, for any reason, I do not come back — and let's face it, I am up in years — I want you to use this key, open the safe, take care of all the paperwork, and give the money to my family. I entrust this key only to you — open the safe only if I don't return."

Sam accepted the key and said he would take care of everything. Abe waved goodbye and went down on the elevator to a waiting cab. No sooner had the cab gone two blocks when Sam raced up next to the cab, out of breath and shouted, "Abe, wait! You gave me the wrong key!"

. . . .

An ad appeared in the classified pages of a major city newspaper. "Original Rembrandt for sale — $100, first come, first served." An art collector read the ad and began to laugh, "Ha! An original Rembrandt for $100. But just for kicks, I think I'll stop over and see what kind of a joke this is."

He arrived at the house and was welcomed by Mrs. Goldberg, who showed him the picture. The art collector was beside himself — the painting, which he thought would be just a fake copy of a Rembrandt, was actually the real thing. It was an authentic original!

He looked at the lady and exclaimed, "Are you sure you only want $100 for this painting?" She nodded that it was all she wanted. The art dealer quickly handed her the cash and the deal was closed.

"Mrs. Goldberg," asked the art dealer. "I must confess — I cheated you. This is an original, worth almost $500,000! Why did you sell it for just $100?"

"Well," explained Mrs. Goldberg, "My communist boss passed away a few weeks ago and stipulated in his will that the painting was to be sold after his death and the money was to be given to the local Communist party."

An American business executive was touring Israel and went into one of Israel's industrial plants. He noticed how their production was humming along with absolute maximum efficiency.

He turned to the plant manager and asked, "Tell me, how do you get such magnificent production?"

The Israeli production engineer smiled and explained, "Well, when we run into a major production problem, we take the laziest man in the factory and put him on that job. In less than 48 hours, he figures out the easiest and quickest way to do the job — then we adopt his method!"

• •

An insurance company instituted a company policy that all their officers and employees had to be of the Catholic faith and all their executives had to come from the ranks. However, a problem arose when one of their best salesmen happened to be a Jew who was also in line for the next executive post. So, the heads of the company, clandestinely, agreed that they would make an effort to convert the Jewish salesman.

"At least," the President said, "We should try."

So they called in a priest and told him the problem. The priest understood and met with the salesman.

The salesman was unaware of what was going on, but he closeted himself in his office with the priest for nearly two hours. Finally the Priest came out, all smiles.

"Well, Father," exclaimed the president of the insurance company, "Were you able to convert him?"

The priest smiled warmly and replied, "Well, not exactly."

"Then what took so long?" questioned the company president.

"Oh," exclaimed the priest, "He sold me a few policies at a great rate!"

. . . .

An old East Side character walked into a bank and spoke with the manager. "How much interest do you charge? I want to arrange a loan."

The manager explained that the bank charged 6% interest on all loans.

"Could I borrow $25?" the man asked.

"Well, I guess you could," the bank manager explained rather hesitatingly. "But you'll have to have some security."

"That I have," the old timer explained and promptly handed over $50,000 in stocks and bonds.

The bank manager was flabbergasted, but he accepted the security and gave the old timer a receipt.

At the end of the year, the old timer was back at the bank and handed the bank manager the $25 he had borrowed, plus $1.50 for the year's interest.

The manager could not contain himself and asked the old timer. "Tell me, if you had all this money in stock and bonds, why in the world did you have to borrow $25?"

"Well," the old timer exclaimed, "Could you think of any other way of getting a safety-deposit vault for $1.50 a year?"

An old timer walked into a bank and said, "I want to take out a loan."

The clerk asked him, "Do you have any collateral, like stocks or bonds? Do you have any money in the bank?"

"Money?" the old timer shrugged, "Why do you think I am here?"

. . . .

An old timer walked into a jewelry store that had a big sign out front which read, "All Watches 25% Off." He happily bought a watch and went home. The very next week, he ran back to the jewelry shop and excitedly declared, "Hey, you know that watch you sold me last week? Its 15 minutes off every day!" The jeweler bristled and snapped, "So what's the problem? Didn't we advertise all watches as being 25% off?"

. . . .

An old timer was penning a letter to the President of the United States when his friend walked in. "I am writing to the President with an idea that will put this nation on its feet, once and for all."

"*Nu*, so what is your plan?" the friend asked.

"It is simple — in today's economy, poor people must pay cash and rich people have unlimited credit. This is wrong. It should be the opposite way around. The poor should have unlimited credit and the rich should pay cash."

"Wait a minute," the friend interjected, "If that be the case, the rich, who will have to extend credit to the poor man, will soon become poor himself. How will that help the economy?"

"Oh, that's simple," explained the old timer. "If the rich man becomes poor, then he will be eligible for unlimited credit; so where's the problem?"

. . . .

An old timer wrote the Internal Revenue Service: "Dear Sirs, I have been unable to sleep all night because I cheated on last year's income tax. Enclosed please find a check for $500. If I find I still can't sleep — I'll send you the rest."

. . . .

An old timer was gasping his last and was speaking to his son. "Abie, my boy, as I leave this world, let me leave you my secret of success — which is honesty and wisdom."

"How would you define those terms, Dad?" little Abie questioned.

The old timer began, "First, honesty means that if you promise a man merchandise, you must deliver it. Even if it means losing money and bankrupting yourself, you must deliver."

The son nodded understandingly and asked, "And how would you interpret wisdom?"

The old man sighed, "Wisdom means you never promise!"

Business was terrible, so Sam called up a customer and pleaded, "Listen, Irving, do you think you can send me a check for the merchandise I sold you last month?" Irving replied, "I'm sorry, Sam, but business is terrible, and I really don't know when I'll be able to send you a check. I hope you understand."

Sam sighed, "Okay. Don't worry! Your credit is still good, I only wish I had ten customers like you."

Irving interjected, "Now wait a minute, now you're making fun of me — especially since I can't pay."

"No, no!" sighed Sam. "That's a compliment! I really wish I had ten customers like you — the trouble is I have over a hundred!"

. . . .

Cohen and Rabinowitz operated a small dress manufacturing business. One day, a young man walked in and said, "Sir, I'm looking for a job. I would like to work for you as a salesman!"

Cohen and Rabinowitz winked to each other. Then Cohen turned to the young man and declared, "What are you — a wise guy? Here you don't start at the top. With us you have to start as a partner!"

. . . .

Cohen called up one of his business clients and snapped, "Max, either you pay me your last bill immediately, or

I will cause you so much trouble you will have to go into bankruptcy!"

Max replied, "Yeah, like what?"

Cohen replied, "If you don't pay up immediately, I will contact all your creditors and tell them you paid me in full!"

. . . .

Cohen called the local police station and said, "Listen, I want a police officer at my office tomorrow morning. There is going to be a murder!"

The police officer replied, "We know, we know. Your partner also called!"

. . . .

Cohen got a call from his bank. "Mr. Cohen, this is the bank manager. We find that you are overdrawn on your account to the tune of $2,000!"

Cohen replied, "*Nu*, so I'm overdrawn. What can I do? I'm a little short this month."

Then bank manager interrupted with, "But Mr. Cohen, you don't understand the seriousness of this call. You are overdrawn by $2,000!"

Cohen snapped back, "Listen, last month how much did I have in my balance?"

"You had more than $10,000," replied the manager.

"*Nu*," Cohen snapped, "Did I call you and make a scene?"

Cohen opened a new fish store and hung out a sign that read, 'Fresh Fish Sold Here Daily.' As his first customer walked in and placed her order, she looked at the sign and said, "Listen, when people see a sign like that, they might wonder, 'Of course the fish you sell here is fresh, otherwise we wouldn't come in,' so why do you have to have the word 'Fresh?'"

"By all means," exclaimed Cohen, who quickly painted out the word 'Fresh.'

A little later, another customer walked in and placed her order. She, too, looked at the sign. "Listen, why do you have to have the sign say 'Here'? Where else would you be selling fish? In China?"

Cohen smiled uneasily and quickly painted out the word 'Here.'

Now the sign simply read, 'Fish Sold Daily.'

Soon, another customer came in and questioned, "Why do you need the word 'Daily' — of course people know you are open every day!"

So he painted out the word 'Daily.'

Still later, another customer came in and asked, "Why do you need the word 'Sold'? People know you don't give the fish away for free!" So he painted out the word 'Sold.'

A little later, another customer walked in and asked, "Why do you have the word 'Fish' on your sign? People can smell it as soon as they walk by!"

So, Cohen picked up the paint-brush again and promptly painted out the word 'Fish'.

A little later in the day, when his wife arrived at the store, she asked, "Why did you paint out the whole sign?" Cohen simply shrugged, "It was a little too wordy."

· ·

Cohen owed Schwartz $100. When Cohen did not pay the debt, Schwartz summoned him to small claims court. Once in court, Schwartz produced ten witnesses to prove that the money was never returned. Cohen came up with twenty witnesses who testified that he had paid back the debt.

Schwartz was so angry, he stood up in court and shouted, "Your honor, to show you what kind of liar he is — I never even loaned him the money!"

· ·

Cohen stormed into the "Snappy Dress Manufacturing Company" and demanded to see the owner, a Mr. Rosenberg.

"Rosenberg," shouted Cohen, "You owe me $5,000 and I want to be paid. I have waited more than six months. It is about time I got my money."

Rosenberg was seated behind his desk and looked at Cohen sadly. "Hymie," he began, "We've been friends for years. And I know I owe you the money. But I don't have it. However, because you were always a true friend and trusted me for the money, I am going to let you in on a secret. I am going into Chapter 11 — I am bankrupt!"

"*Gevald!*" screeched Cohen. "What about my money?"

"Don't worry," exclaimed Rosenberg. "Because of our friendship, I am going to make you a preferred creditor!"

"That's good?" questioned Cohen.

"That's very good," Rosenberg replied. "You see, you know now. The others won't know until next week!"

. . . .

Cohen took out a large insurance policy on his business. As he affixed his name to the policy, he joked to the insurance man, "So tell me, since I am now insured, if my place should burn down tonight, what would I get?"

The insurance agent smiled warmly and replied, "About ten years."

. . . .

Cohen walked into one of the larger banks on Wall Street and asked to see the president of the bank.

"He's a very busy man," the secretary said.

"Well, I have an investment problem, and I think he is the only one who could solve my problem." Cohen exclaimed.

She smiled and said, "Well, if it is a big investment problem, I probably could disturb him."

She ushered Cohen into the bank president's office. The president of the bank promptly opened a bottle of scotch and offered a glass to Cohen. They sat for a few minutes making the bottle disappear. Then the bank president said,

"I understand you have an investment problem. Well, that's what we are here for. Now, what's your problem?"

Cohen gulped down his last drink, which drained the bottle, and said, "My problem is I don't have any money to invest!"

. . . .

Cohen was a pretzel salesman. He never missed a day of work in twenty years. He would always stand on the corner, rain or shine, shouting, "Hot pretzels below cost!"

When one sympathetic stranger would buy a pretzel from him, Cohen would sigh, "I lose money on every pretzel I sell," and he would frown bitterly at the pretzels.

One day, a passerby got curious. "Tell me," he asked, "If you're losing so much money with each pretzel you sell, why don't you quit?"

"Quit?" Cohen sighed sadly, "How else would I make a living?"

. . . .

Cohen was a wealthy Garment Center manufacturer and had made a 'nothing' business into one of the largest clothing firms in the country. As the years passed, Cohen was near his end. He called his lawyer to his side and said, "Sol, I want to make a stipulation in my will that every employee who has worked for me for twenty-five years or more is to get a special bequest of $25,000 each."

The attorney looked at him strangely, "Sam, you didn't go into business until ten years ago…"

"I know," gasped Cohen, "But think how nice it will look in the newspapers!"

· ·

Cohen was at death's door and he sent for his lawyer to make his last will and testament. Cohen's wife stayed in the room as the lawyer took dictation from Cohen.

Cohen took a deep breath and said, "I want you to collect money from those who owe me. For example, Shloimy Goldfadden owes me $200. Irving Lefkowitz owes me $500."

His wife sat in a corner biting her nails and uttered, "Oh, what a wonderful man. See how organized and sharp his mind is until the very end."

Then Cohen continued, "And I want you to pay Seymour Jacobs, my old customer, the $1,000 he loaned me some years ago."

The wife stood up and shouted, "*Gevald!* See, he's lost his mind!"

· ·

Cohen was complaining about business to his friend. "Business is so rotten, that every day I open my store, I lose $200."

"So how do you live?" his friend asked.

"I'm keeping closed two days a week, and on $400, I can live!" he replied.

. . . .

Cohen was frantic. For three weeks he hadn't been able to do a thing with his business because he had forgotten the combination to the safe. His partner had gone on a tour of Europe and could not be reached. All the firm's books were locked in the safe and the operating capital was likewise in the safe.

Then suddenly, as if by mental telepathy, Cohen received a call from his partner in London.

"*Oy, vey,*" exclaimed Cohen, "That safe is costing me the business. I forgot the combination and I can't get to anything. Tell me the combination, quick!"

"Alright, listen close," his partner calmly stated, "Turn left once and twice right."

"But how about the numbers — where do I stop?" Cohen pleaded.

"Numbers? Stop? It doesn't matter! The lock's been broken for almost a year!"

. . . .

Cohen was holding his head when his partner walked in. "What happened?" his partner, Goldberg, asked.

"What happened? I just realized that we sold Rabinowitz 100 coats from stock and the shipping clerk forgot to get a receipt. If I ask him now for a receipt, he will deny he ever got the coats, and we will never get our money."

Goldberg smiled with reassurance, "Listen, it's so simple. All we have to do is send him a bill for 300 coats."

"Are you crazy," snapped Cohen. "All he took was 100!"

"I know, I know," laughed Goldberg. "But when Rabinowitz gets the bill for 300 coats, he will write back that you are an idiot because all he took was 100 coats! And *shoen* — you will have the acknowledgment we need!"

· ·

Cohen was *nouveau riche* and now had money he never dreamed of. With his newfound wealth he purchased nothing but the best for his family. One day, his daughter was taken ill with appendicitis and went to a hospital. As the surgeon approached, he declared, "There is nothing to worry about, Mr. Cohen. It is merely a routine operation. We'll be giving her a local anesthetic." Cohen interrupted, "No, no, doctor. Get her the imported stuff, I can afford it!"

· ·

Cohen was operating a funeral parlor and things were very bad. His wife tried to console him when she noticed someone coming into the place. She turned to her husband and whispered, "Here comes a customer, cheer up and look sad!"

Cohen was talking to a friend. "I hear you failed in business."

The second fellow sighed, "That's true."

"What happened?" Cohen questioned.

"Too much advertising," he sighed once more.

"Impossible," Cohen snapped. "I know you, and you never spent a cent on advertising."

"I know," sighed his friend, "Not me, but my competitor!"

. . . .

Cohen was trying to describe a former partner. "Let me tell you, he was so crooked, even the wool he pulled over people's eyes was 50% polyester!"

. . . .

Cohen was walking on the Lower East Side when one of the clothing store hawks grabbed him by the shoulder and said, "Come into my shop — let me sell you a suit."

Cohen smiled and said, "Listen, I don't need a suit! I have a dozen suits at home."

The clothing storeowner smiled uneasily and quipped, "Bring them in and I'll make you a partner!"

. . . .

Cohen was wringing his hands in despair when his friend Goldberg walked in.

"I'm just about bankrupt," Cohen lamented. "I owe everybody."

Goldberg tried to console his friend and said, "Listen, it could be worse."

Cohen bristled, "How could it be worse?"

Goldberg sighed, "I might have been one of your creditors."

. . . .

Cohen wasn't a bad landlord; it was just that Goldberg was a tenant who was an artist and had not paid his rent in months. Finally, in disgust, Cohen went up to Goldberg and snapped, "Either I get my rent or out you go!"

Goldberg replied, "You don't realize what you are doing. I am a great artist! Why, sometime in the future, people will pass this miserable apartment and sigh, 'See? This is the place where the famous painter, Goldberg, once lived.'"

To which Cohen retorted, "And if I don't get the rent by tonight, they will start saying it tomorrow!"

. . . .

Cohen went into a shoe store to purchase a pair of shoes. The shoe salesman measured his foot and smiled, "Okay, you take a size 10-EEE."

Cohen looked at the salesman and said, "Please give me a size 8-EE."

The salesman smiled uneasily, remeasured the foot and said,

"But Mr. Cohen, your foot measures a size 10-EEE, why do you want a size 8-EE?"

The old timer sighed, "Listen, my friend, my business is terrible, every day I lose a fortune. The only pleasure I get is when I come home at night and take off my tight shoes... please, a size 8-EE!"

• •

Cohen, the owner of the Snappy Dressing Manufacturing Company, decided to go to Switzerland to try his hand at mountain climbing.

He purchased a few thousand dollars' worth of equipment and ordered the best guide money could buy. No sooner did his plane land, that he set out for the Alps. The guide led him up craggy turns and ice-covered trails. Cohen was doing well. Then, suddenly, there was a thunderous sound. An avalanche! He fell into a crevice in the mountain and was helplessly wedged there. No matter how much his guide tried, it was almost impossible to free him.

"Mr. Cohen," his guide called down, "I'll go for help!" and he scampered down the mountain.

A Red Cross emergency rescue team made their way up the mountain. Finally, they reached the spot. The rescue team made their way into the crevice and prepared to drop a safety line. In order to determine Cohen's condition, the rescue team called out, "Mr. Cohen, how are you?"

Cohen called back, "Cold, but hanging on! Who's that up there?"

The rescue team replied, "This is the Red Cross."

Cohen called back quickly, "At a time like this? Listen, I already gave at the office!"

. . . .

Dave Breger, the accountant, was talking to a client who looked a little depressed.

"What's the matter?" Breger asked.

"I'm a little annoyed," the client explained. "My wife woke up this morning and told me she dreamt she married a multi-millionaire!"

"Boy, are you lucky!" exclaimed Breger, "My wife dreams that in the daytime!"

. . . .

For years, the sideshow strong-man had awed crowds by squeezing a lemon dry, then offering $1,000 to anyone who could get another drop out of it.

Nobody paid much attention when a wispy little man in one audience dared challenge him. The strong man first squeezed the lemon until it was little more than a pulp, then handed it to the little man, who not only squeezed out another drop, but also got almost a cup of juice!

"Amazing," the strong man conceded. "What kind of work do you do?"

"I'm with the Internal Revenue Service," the little man replied.

MONEY & BUSINESS

Goldberg and Cohen were partners in a dress house in New York's Garment Center. They were moderately successful, but in recent months, they began to feel the pinch of the economy. They were on the verge of bankruptcy with tremendous inventory.

Then, as luck would have it, a big Texan representing one of Texas' leading department stores walked in, saw their stock, and said he would take all their dresses. They were saved! But the Texan added. "I have to go back to our office in Texas to make sure the order can be firm. If you don't hear from me by Friday at 3:00 PM the deal is set. Ship all the dresses."

The two partners watched the mail every day and, thank goodness, no letter and no phone calls. Then came Friday. They were nervous wrecks. This order could save their business.

It was five minutes to 3:00 PM as they stood by the phone praying they would not get the call. Then, just one minute before 3:00 PM, there was a knock on the door.

Both grew pale. Cohen barely made it to the door and discovered it was Western Union with a telegram. He opened the envelope slowly, as Goldberg gingerly came to the door. Cohen finally breathed a sigh of relief and shouted, "Goldberg! It's good news! It's really good news! It's from your wife. She says someone crashed into your new Cadillac and it is in total ruin!"

- -

Goldberg was a sly operator from the old school. Since he was a little short of funds, he went into bank to seek

48

a $200 loan. The bank manager very politely told him that since his credit wasn't established, the best they could do was to give him $100.

A few months later, he got a notice from the bank that he had not made any payments on the loan. In anger, Goldberg stormed into the bank, cornered the bank manager and snapped, "Listen, I came in for a $200 loan. All you could afford was $100. So, that means you still owe me $100! So, why all the commotion? Let's just call it even!"

• •

Goldberg was contemplating science when his partner came in. "Irving," he exclaimed. "I was just thinking, you know this suit I'm wearing? Just think — the wool came from Australia, the cloth was woven in New England and the thread comes from India. The suit was made in New York City, and I bought it in California!"

"So, what's so remarkable about that?" exclaimed his friend.

"It's simply amazing how much money so many people can earn from something I haven't even paid for yet!"

• •

Goldberg was getting ready to close his shop, when a woman walked in and asked, "I'd like to see something in sweaters."

Goldberg smiled and reached for a box. He spread a few samples on the counter and waited. The woman looked at each carefully then sighed, "These aren't exactly the color I wanted."

He smiled and then brought down several more boxes. She opened each box, spread the sweaters all over the counter, then sighed, "The colors are right, but I would like one with a little more warmth."

Goldberg took down a dozen more boxes and she went through each one carefully. An hour passed, when she finally said, "These aren't quite what I had in mind. But don't let it bother you, I was just looking for my sister-in-law."

Goldberg smiled, started to fold up the pile of sweaters, then said, "Lady, I'll make you a present of a dozen sweaters if you'll answer me just one question. Tell me, if you were just looking for your sister-in-law, what made you think you'd ever find her in one of these boxes?"

. . . .

Goldberg, who operated his own shop in the Garment Center, decided to go to night school to improve his use of the English language.

One day, when he returned to his office, he realized one of his customers owed him a sum of money, and the payment, long overdue, had still not arrived. He sat down and began to write a proper letter following every rule the teacher had shown him, including getting to the point immediately, and using proper idiomatic expressions.

After he finished typing his letter, he brought it to his teacher to double check to make certain everything was according to form.

The teacher read the letter, then commented, "Mr. Goldberg, this is an excellent letter and you held to every rule I taught you. However, there are a few minor corrections. For example, the word 'lousy' is not spelled with a 'E', the word 'filthy' is spelled with an 'H' and there is no 'C' in 'skunk.' Other than that, the letter is perfect!"

⋯⋯⋯⋯⋯⋯⋯⋯⋯⋯⋯⋯⋯⋯⋯⋯⋯⋯

Goldberg's clothing store was running a fantastic sale on men's suits. People started lining up in front of the store at daybreak. Around 9:00 AM, a man walked toward the front of the line, but before he could even break into the line, a few of those who had already waited for hours grabbed him by the collar and shoved him toward the back.

The old timer brushed himself off and tried to break into the front of the line once more. Again, the others on the line grabbed him and shoved him to the back of the line.

Finally, a cop walked over and asked, "What's going on here?"

The old timer brushed himself off once more and exclaimed, "If they do that once more, I'm not opening the store!"

⋯⋯⋯⋯⋯⋯⋯⋯⋯⋯⋯⋯⋯⋯⋯⋯⋯⋯

Harrigan and Schwartz were partners for years, but they secretly envied each other. As soon as Harrigan got something new, Schwartz got two! If Harrigan got a new

Cadillac, Schwartz went out and bought a Lincoln Continental *and* a Mustang.

Finally, one day, Schwartz decided to give Harrigan the business, and put a telephone in his car. Riding around in his chauffeured limousine, he called his office and told his secretary to have Harrigan call him on his new car phone.

Meanwhile Harrigan, having heard that Schwartz was going to put in a car phone, also had one put in his car. When his secretary told him Schwartz called, he promptly dialed Schwartz's car phone from his own car phone.

"Yes, this is Schwartz! Of course, you know you're calling me on my new car telephone! I'm driving on the West Side Drive while you're talking..."

Harrigan replied, "Well, for your information, I also have a phone in my car, and I'm calling you while I'm driving in the middle of the East River Drive."

"What?" exclaimed Schwartz, "I can't hear you."

Harrigan repeated, "I said, I'm also calling you from my car telephone."

"I can't hear you," shouted Schwartz once more.

"Whatsamatter, are you deaf?" screamed Harrigan.

"No," Schwartz replied, "I couldn't hear you because my other phone is ringing!"

. . . .

Herbie Ungeshtopped was attending a stockholder's meeting. The president of the corporation, a hefty, pompous individual, *groggered* on for hour-after-hour, talking about the operation of the firm. As the stockholders became bored, they began to mutter to each other.

"Please, please, ladies and gentlemen," the president exclaimed. "I can hardly hear myself!"

"Don't worry," shouted Herbie, "You're not missing much!"

- -

In a panic, Finkel exclaimed to the police on the phone, "I want to report a stolen car."

"Yes sir," replied the officer, "When was the car stolen?"

"Sometime early last week," replied Finkle.

"Last week?" gasped the officer. "Why did you wait so long to report it missing?"

"Well," replied Finkel, "For one thing, my partner was in it…"

- -

In a case where a company was trying to collect a bill, this old timer wrote them back, "Dear Sir, I think you should know that we have a unique system of how we pay our creditors. We have three creditor classifications. We divide our creditors accordingly:

Class A — Those we pay promptly.

Class B — Those we pay in the near future.

Class C — Those who have to wait and wait and wait.

"Therefore, in consideration of the friendly tone of your letter, we are promoting you from class C to class B."

· ·

In the Garment Center a manufacturer found himself stuck with a heavy stock of pants in a certain style that was very popular during the summer. But what good is keeping all that stock throughout the winter when they might be out of style next year? He was ready to sell the lot for just the cost of the material.

Suddenly, he got an idea. He looked over his books and found one retailer whom he knew was not the most honest of men. So he wrapped up ten pairs of the pants and shipped them with a cover letter in which he wrote: "I'm enclosing nine pairs of pants for $10.95 a pair."

He figured that the dishonest retailer would discover the ten pairs of pants and the temptation of obtaining ten pairs when he was only being billed for nine, would be too much to resist. He felt he would have gotten a check back immediately. The small loss he would have to take was well worth it. If it worked with this fellow, he would try it with others.

But instead of getting a check by return mail, he got a letter, which read: "Dear Mr. Teitelbaum, We have examined the nine pairs of pants you shipped and found them excellent as to price and quality. However, since the season is over, and I don't know what will be next year, I'm returning the merchandise to you."

Enclosed in the package were nine pairs of pants.

In the Garment Center a supplier shouted at a manufacturer, "Listen, Abe, I've done more for you than your mother!"

The manufacturer snapped back, "Oh yeah, how?"

"She carried you for nine months; I've been carrying you for fifteen!" he retorted.

• •

Irving Rabinowitz prided himself on running one of the most efficient laundry businesses in Brooklyn. He had a habit of walking through the plant as often as possible to make sure he was getting a full day's work out of his employees.

One day, passing through the packaging department, he saw a young man sitting on one of the tables smoking a cigarette and reading a newspaper. Irving walked over to the youth and demanded, "How much do you earn a week?"

The youth stood up and replied, "$200 a week, sir!"

Irving put his hand in his pocket pulled out two crisp $100 bills and handed them to the youth, snapping, "Here's your week's pay. Now get out!"

After the youth left, Irving called over the foreman and shouted, "I blame you for that kid goofing off. How could you hire such a worker who just sits around like that?"

The foreman stammered, "I, I, I didn't hire him. He works for the delivery company and was waiting to take the next load!"

I rving walked into his partner's office and exclaimed, "Cohen, I have something to tell you. You know Goldberg, our inside salesman? Well, I have absolute proof that he is stealing from the business!" Cohen grew angry and said, "Send Goldberg to my office immediately!"

In a few minutes, Goldberg was in the office.

"Tell me Goldberg, how much do you get here each week?" Goldberg, a little frightened, replied, "I make $75 a week."

"Hardly enough!" Cohen exclaimed. "Tell the bookkeeper to put you down for a $100 raise!"

Goldberg thanked the boss, walked out and promptly told Irving the partner that he just got a $100 raise.

Irving ran back to Cohen. "Are you crazy? I just told you the man is stealing us blind and you give him a $100 a week raise!"

Cohen smiled, "Send Goldberg back."

In a few minutes, Goldberg was back in the office.

"I made a Mistake, Goldberg, when I gave you the $100 raise," said Cohen. "Make that $200, for a total of $275 a week!" he ordered. Goldberg thanked the boss and ran out to tell Irving once more.

Irving ran back into the office and shouted, "I am convinced you are out of your mind. Here I tell you the man is a thief, and you give him a $200 weekly raise?"

"Of course," replied Cohen. "The man is a scoundrel, and he will be fired at the end of this week. But, when he is fired, I want him to know he is not losing $75 a week, but $275!"

It is claimed that the Goldberg brothers, Max, Norman, and Hyman, invented the home air conditioning system. When they demonstrated the system to a big manufacturer, the manufacturer said, "I'll give you $5 million for the system."

The brothers said, "We'll sell it to you on one condition: our name has to be on every air conditioner made." The manufacturer thought for a moment, then said, "But to put 'Goldberg' on every air conditioner...I don't think will go over very well in certain parts of the country. You know, there are some people out there who do not look kindly on Jewish names. It could hurt sales."

The brothers thought for a moment and said, "Okay, how about just using out first names?"

The manufacturer smiled and said, "Max, I can see no harm in that. How about you Norm, and how do you feel about it, Hy?" They all agreed.

So, now every air conditioner made carries the names of the three brothers who developed the system. Look on your own air conditioner and you will see, "MAX, HI, and NORM."

· ·

It was in a cemetery and the poor woman was sobbing hysterically. An elderly man passed by and tried to comfort her.

"Someone closely related to you?" he mused.

She continued sobbing.

"Your sister, maybe?" the old timer persisted, trying to help.

The woman continued sobbing.

"A daughter...?" the old man asked softly.

The woman looked up with red-rimmed eyes and explained, "My husband!"

The old timer looked at the tombstone, which read, "Sarah Foofnik."

"How could this be your husband?" he questioned.

"How!" she exclaimed, "He was in bankruptcy and everything was in my name!"

· ·

Leibowitz called up one of his business associates and asked, "*Nu*, Sam, did you get my check?"

The voice on the other end of the phone replied, "Yes, twice! Once from you, and once marked 'Insufficient Funds' from the bank!"

· ·

Morris Kuchelman was called down to the Internal Revenue Service for a tax audit. The old timer appeared with a million little slips of paper and laid them out before the revenue agent. The inspector tried to decipher the maze of paper and snapped, "Look, Mr. Kuchelman, this is no good. If you want credit for all these deductions, you have to show me actual receipts, invoices, inventory lists, your income, expenses, donations, contributions, etcetera."

Kuchelman looked up and snapped, "Listen, mister, that

information I don't even give my accountant, why should I give to you, a total stranger?"

. . . .

My wife recently got a bill from a department store, which said, "This bill is now one year old."

So she wrote back, "Happy birthday!"

. . . .

One day, Hymie said to his wife, "You heard about Shloimy Upgelozzen? Since his business went bankrupt and he lost his money, he lost half of his friends!"

"And what about the other half?" his wife asked.

"They don't know he lost his money yet!"

. . . .

One day, Rabinowitz boasted to his friend Sam, "I just picked up a bargain on 100 cases of Cuban cigars. Now, since you are the best salesman in the world, I want you to get the best price for these cigars that you possibly can."

Sam acknowledged the compliment and took a few dozen cigars with him. Customer after customer tried a cigar and threw them back at Sam. The cigars were terrible. Finally, after a week of trying, Sam gave up and returned to his main office. Rabinowitz met him at the door.

"Well, Sam, the best salesman in the world, how'd you make

out?" Sam looked at Rabinowitz and declared, "Max, I have a confession to make. I'm not the world's best salesman."

"You're not?" Rabinowitz exclaimed. "If you're not, then who is?" he asked jocularly.

"The guy who sold those cigars to you!"

. . . .

One day, Shloimy came home from work in the tailor shop. "*Oy*, am I happy, I am so happy!"

"So tell me, why are you so happy?" asked his wife.

"Remember last winter we discovered a leak in the cellar on Sunday...?"

"*Nu*? So tell me!" pleaded his wife.

"And you remember, we called a plumber to hurry up and come over to fix the leak?..."

"*Nu*...nu...so tell me already," she pleaded.

"And he didn't come for over three hours...and the basement flooded."

"So tell me already," his wife sighed.

"So...he just brought a suit in to be altered and he said he needs it for tonight!"

. . . .

One of the larger business concerns in New York City sent out notices to their creditors which read, "SECOND

NOTICE!" Under that heading, they said legal action was about to be taken.

One of the creditors contacted the treasurer of the company. "Listen, we just sent through the amount we owe your firm, but I have to tell you, we never received your first notice. If we did, we would have sent you a check immediately!"

The treasurer sent back a note, which read, "Thank you for your remittance. By the way, we never send out first notices, only second notices. We find that to be more efficient. Besides, you should see how much postage we save!"

· ·

Rosenberg owned a small delicatessen on the Lower East Side. His brother operated a small tourist bureau in the back of the delicatessen out of which he sold cheap tickets to Israel. One day, Rosenberg got a call to come down to the Internal Revenue Service office for a tax examination.

"Mr. Rosenberg," sighed the clerk, "You own a small store. All you sell is hot dogs and corn beef sandwiches, yet on your tax return you are claiming eighty-nine trips to Israel as a business expense. How come?"

Rosenberg smiled warmly and exclaimed, "We deliver!"

· ·

Sadie phoned the bakery and said, "Mr. Schwartz, I sent my son for two pounds of cookies and you only sent a half pound. Have you checked your scales?"

The baker replied. "My scales are perfect. Tell me, have you weighed your little boy?"

. . . .

Sadie met an old friend and they began talking about their children. "*Oy* do I have *tzurus!* Problems like you wouldn't know!" she began.

"What kind of problems?" the friend asked.

"It's my son-in-law. *Oy*, is that a no-goodnik!"

"What's so terrible about your son-in-law?" the friend questioned.

"What's so terrible? — He can't gamble! That's what's so terrible," Sadie shouted.

"If he can't gamble, that's so terrible?" the friend questioned.

"Of course!" Sadie exclaimed, "He can't gamble — but he does!"

. . . .

Sadie was telling her son how a swindler sold her shares in an oil well stock that wasn't worth the paper it was printed on.

"Ma," exclaimed the son, "Why didn't you call me? You know I have a number of friends in the stock market. I could have checked out that stock for you in a minute. Why didn't you call me?"

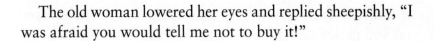

The old woman lowered her eyes and replied sheepishly, "I was afraid you would tell me not to buy it!"

. . . .

Sam and Abe were partners in a dry goods store for years. Each trusted the other as far as he could throw him. One day, a gypsy came into the store and told them he had a magic fluid that would turn black automatically if one of the partners took money from the cash register without the others knowledge. The two men decided to each buy a bottle and promptly put their initials on the bottles for identification.

It was agreed that the two bottles would remain on a shelf in full view, so that should one be dishonest, the other would know immediately. But, as it was, the fluids stayed clear for almost a week.

Meanwhile, Abe decided to play a practical joke and emptied Sam's bottle of fluid and filled it with black ink. He didn't say a word, but merely went about his business as usual, hoping Sam would discover the black fluid and then begin protestations all over the place.

Later on, Abe had to go to the basement to check on something. Suddenly, Abe noticed his bottle had turned black. He turned pale.

Seeing that Sam was out of sight, he promptly emptied the contents of the bottle into the sink and refilled it with clear water.

"Hmmm," he muttered, "That gypsy was right!"

Sam and Abe were partners in the Garment Center for years and decided to take a long-needed vacation together. On the way to the airport, Sam turned and gasped, "Abe, I just realized we closed the place and I left the safe open!"

Abe smiled, understanding, "Sam, why are you worried... we're both here!"

. . . .

Sam and his wife Sarah ran a dry goods store on the Lower East Side. For years, the two old-timers worked around the clock to keep the store open all hours. With the meager money they earned, they were able to send their son to college.

Now, finally, their son Sheldon was graduating with a degree in business administration. When the son came into the store, he exclaimed, "Dad, we're going to run this business the way big businesses are run!" The old man was jubilant. After all, his son's college education was not going to waste.

"*Nu*, Sheldon," the old timer asked, "What must I do?"

"Well," replied Sheldon, "First we have to hire an accountant. Your books are in terrible order — I can't make heads or tails out of them."

"Okay," the old timer agreed, and they hired a fancy accountant to set up a new set of books. After the first week of wading through the pile of bills and sales slips, the accountant ran to the old timer and announced, "Mr. Goldberg, I hate to say this, but according to the figures, you're bankrupt!" The old man was destroyed. He went home that night and sat sadly at the dinner table, "All those years and now we're bankrupt..."

His wife asked, "How come all of a sudden?"

"The accountant says, and he knows," he sighed.

"Listen," the old lady said softly, "All these years we made a living. We were able to send Sheldon to college. We had food in the icebox and we paid the rent. All from the same store. Nothing has changed over the years except the accountant. It's so simple, fire the accountant and we'll be back on a paying basis!"

. . . .

Sam graduated college and now had a degree in Business Administration. Upon graduation, his father took him into the family business.

The first day in the office his father announced. "Sam, my boy, I'm putting you in charge of the office. What you say goes! You went to college to learn this, so now your word is law."

The son smiled and declared, "Well, Pop, the first thing we must do is clean off the top of your desk. You got bills and papers here from the year 2 BCE!"

The old man was a little taken aback, but he stuck to his word. "Okay, you can clean everything off my desk, tear up every shred of paper, destroy every ancient bill, anything you want — but first make a copy of everything!"

. . . .

Sam Rabinowitz was an honest man, but had the habit, which got most of his vendors angry, of post-dating his checks. That meant he would write an advanced date on a check to his creditors. This would make it impossible for them to cash the check without waiting a few weeks.

One day, he died. Since he was a good fellow, his creditors chipped in to purchase a tombstone for him. It read, "Here lies Sam Rabinowitz — died September 10th, as of October 1st."

* * *

Sam Shlemozzel exclaimed to a friend, "Boy, has my brother Louie got an item to put on the market."

"What kind of item your brother's got?" the friend asked.

"Well, Louie has a watch that never needs to be wound or repaired. In fact, it has no hands, no sweep second dial, and even no face."

"But how can you tell time?"

"That's easy," exclaimed Shlemozzel. "You ask somebody!"

* * *

Sam was down on his luck. When you saw him walk the streets in his threadbare suit, compassion filled you. Then one day, he appeared on the street in a handsome new suit of clothes and stepped into a brand-new Lincoln Continental, with a chauffeur at the wheel.

"Sam," his old friend called out, "I don't understand it. Just a few months ago you were so down on your luck I was afraid to talk to you, and today you look like a millionaire."

Sam beamed, "Well, you see, I was in cloaks and suits for

years. And one day, I met a fellow who I decided to go into business with."

"Wait a minute," his friend interrupted. "How could you go into a partnership? You didn't have a penny to your name."

"I know," exclaimed Sam, "I had the experience, and my partner had $50,000."

"Aha," exclaimed his friend, "And the business was a success?"

"No, actually," explained Sam. "In fact, we dissolved just last week."

"So how come you look so wealthy?" his friend asked.

"Well, now my partner has the experience, and I have the $50,000!"

- -

Sam was pouring over some papers, then sighed to his wife, "Sadie, you go to sleep, I'll probably be up all night, I have to fill out my income tax report."

Sadie paused at the door and sighed, "Look, dear, why don't you just write the truth and get a good night's rest?"

- -

Sam was sitting on a park bench with a friend and commented, "You know, if I could only get someone to invest $5,000 in a new idea I have. I could really make some money."

His friend asked, "*Nu,* so tell me how much could you make?" Sam sighed, "About $5,000!"

·   —

Sam Yachenflaster was an extraordinary fund-raiser for the shul and all the local charities. It was said he could squeeze blood out of a stone. But as it must come to all men, Sam passed away, and through a clerical error, instead of going to Heaven, his soul was sent to the other place. When the angels in Heaven began to check their books, they realized what had happened and called downstairs.

"Listen, through a clerical error, you got Sam Yachenflaster. He belongs up here," the angels said. Then they added, "By the way, how is he handling all the heat down there — you know, he wasn't a very strong person."

"What are you talking about?" snapped the voice on the line. "This guy's great! He's been here only two days, and he's already raised more than $1,000 for a new air-conditioning system!"

·   —

Sam, a world-famous tailor and Garment Center magnate, was invited to Washington to dine with the President. It was a big moment in his life. When he returned, one of his friends ran to him and exclaimed, "Nu Sam, so tell me what kind of a man is the President of the United States?"

Without batting an eye, he said, "A 39-short!"

am's business was bad. Every day he would lay off two men here and two men there. Yet, no matter what he did, things got worse. As time went on, he passed away of a broken heart. At his funeral, his partner was standing next to the body. Just then, Sam sat up and asked his partner, "Joe, how many men are carrying me?"

Joe replied, "Six of our most trusted employees."

Sam shook his head sadly, "Better lay off two!"

• •

hapiro met his friend Moshe, and exclaimed, "Moshe, whenever I see you, I'm reminded of Goldberg, may he rest in peace."

"What are you talking," snapped Moshe, "I'm not a bit like him!"

"Yes you are! He owed me money also!"

• •

hapiro wanted to borrow some money from his friend and approached him. "Listen, Sam, could you loan me a few hundred until business gets a little better?"

Sam explained, "Listen, I'd love to, but you know as well as I that loans make enemies."

Shapiro sighed, "I know — I know — but we never were very good friends to start with."

Shapiro went to his old friend Leibowitz and declared, "Solomon, I have a small favor to ask of you. I needed some money, so I went to the bank, and they said they would give me the money if you would sign this note."

Leibowitz smiled, "Irving, my dear friend, why do you go to a stranger for money? Go back to the bank, if they sign the note — I'll give you the money!"

. . . .

Shmuel Goldberg had started life out as a pushcart peddler. The years were good to him, and he eventually opened up his own junk business. As the years passed, he went on to become one of the wealthiest iron and steel dealers in the country. He sent his son to the best schools. However, while at college, his son changed his name from Goldberg to Murphy. He told his father it would be good for business.

So, the old man also changed his name to Murphy. Now, when anybody calls the firm and says they want to speak to Mr. Murphy, the operator asks. "Which one, Shmuel Goldberg or Irving Goldberg?"

. . . .

Somebody told me that President Bush once called a Wall Street stockbroker friend and said, "I think the economy will be picking up from now on. In fact, if I weren't President, I'd be buying stock right now."

The stockbroker replied, "George, if you weren't President, I'd be buying stock, too!"

Sophie had reached her 62nd birthday and was now eligible for Social Security. However, when she got her first check, she did not understand what it was. She phoned her daughter, "Sadie, I got a green sheet of paper from the government with numbers on it. What is this?"

The daughter laughed and replied, "Ma — that's your Social Security check. Just sign it and cash it!"

"How do I sign it? Where do I sign it?" the old lady was so confused. "Ma, all you do is turn the check to the back and sign it like when you sign a letter to me."

The old lady breathed a sigh of relief and hung up. Then she went to the bank with the check and signed it, "Love, Mama."

. . . .

Things were generally bad and one Garment Center manufacturer called in one of his showroom salesmen and said, "Sam, you'll have to go on the road to get some orders."

"You're crazy, Abe," the salesman explained. "Nobody is ordering these days."

"Listen Sam," the boss explained, "If you're half the salesman I think you are, you'll go on the road and cry real tears in front of a prospective customer. Tell them you have a family to support. Tell them your children are starving, that your wife is sick, and they are ready to foreclose on your mortgage. Give them the whole *megillah*. You know what I mean. And, if necessary, cry real tears. Wear an old worn-out suit. You can do it. Give it the old college try, Sam."

Sam was reluctant but went on the road anyway. He was gone for six months and not one single order came in. Finally, he returned to New York and met with his boss.

"Sam," his boss stammered, "Six months on the road and not one order. Did you cry like I told you?"

Sam sighed, "I sure did! But, I told you, business was bad. Nobody wanted dresses. But," he continued, "I did manage to pick up $2,000 in donations for my family!"

. . . .

Three partners met at their office on a Sunday morning to go over their books. After they got into the building, they discovered the elevators weren't running.

"But we're on the 45th floor," exclaimed the oldest partner. "We can't walk all the way up!"

"Don't worry," exclaimed the second partner, "We'll tell each other sad stories as we walk, and we'll feel good by companionship." The third partner agreed and began to tell his sad story. Oh, what a tragic story it was!

As they walked up each flight of stairs, the story got sadder and sadder. But they felt better and didn't mind the hike. As the second partner began his tale of woe, they passed the 22nd floor. The story was so sad, each had tears in his eyes. They were breathing hard as they reached the 45th floor, but they finally made it.

Then the two partners turned to the senior partner and said, "And what is your sad story? Tell it while we catch our breath."

The old timer shrugged, looked sadly at the other two and declared, "Gentlemen, my sad story is — I forgot the key!"

. . . .

Toddler Property Laws: If I like it, it's mine. If it's in my hand, it's mine. If I can take it from you, it's mine. If it looks like mine, it is mine. If I think it's mine, it's mine. If it's yours and I steal it, it's mine. If I'm building something, all the pieces are mine. Whoops! Sorry, I goofed — I thought I was reading the Toddler Property Laws. Nope! I was reading from the IRS Tax Manual.

. . . .

Two business men were arguing over an unpaid bill. "My friend," exclaimed the first fellow. "Your bill is over six months old. When will you pay me what you owe me?"

The second fellow exclaimed, quite annoyed, "Look, business is bad, and I simply can't pay you."

When nothing else would help, the first fellow brought the debtor to a rabbi and pleaded, "Rabbi, this fellow owes me money and doesn't pay."

"Rabbi," the second fellow explained, "Business is bad, and I'm hard pressed for money."

The first fellow snapped, "He's a liar! He's been saying the same thing for the past six months!"

The second fellow looked hurt as he exclaimed, "I'm not

a liar. I did just what I said for the past six months. How can he call me a liar; did I pay him?"

. . . .

Two car dealers were holding a conversation.

"*Nu*, Sam, so how's business?"

"Well, I just sold my dealership and came away with half a million dollars."

"That's incredible. Everybody I talk to tells me they're losing money!"

"That's also true. Don't forget, I went in with $1 million!"

. . . .

Two fellows meet in the street. "Shloimy, it's so good to see you again. So what's new?"

Shloimy shrugs, "I'm thinking of trading in my old car for a new one."

The first follow asks, "How many miles do you have on it?"

"About 98,000 miles."

"Wow, so many miles?" his friend gasps. "You'll get next to nothing for it on a trade-in!"

"But it still runs," Shloimy exclaims.

"Listen," his friend whispers to him, "My cousin knows how to turn back the odometer in a car. It's a little illegal, but he can turn it back so that it will show very low mileage.

Then you trade it in and can get a good price for the car. Let me have my cousin get in touch with you."

The cousin gets in touch with Shloimy and turns back his car's odometer.

A few weeks later, the friend meets Shloimy at a parking lot and he is still driving his old car.

"How come you didn't get your new car?"

Shloimy shrugged, "Why should I, the car is practically brand new! It has so few miles on it!"

. . . .

Two fellows were discussing the present-day economy. "Business is terrible," said the first fellow. "Monday, I sold one suit. Tuesday I sold nothing for a whole day. And Wednesday was even worse than Tuesday!"

"How could you say that?" his friend asked. "If Monday you sold one suit, and Tuesday you sold nothing, how could Wednesday be worse than Tuesday?"

His friend sighed, "On Wednesday, the fellow who bought the suit on Monday returned it!"

. . . .

Two fellows were talking. "Sam, how do you like the second-hand car I sold you last month?"

The second fellow sighed, "*Oy* is that a car! It goes so fast, I want you to know, last week when I was speeding on

an open stretch of highway in Brooklyn, I was caught by a foot-patrol man!"

. . . .

Two Garment Center manufacturers were talking about how successful they were. "I want you to know we recently got an offer for 10,000 garments from Alexanders!"

The other fellow snapped, "I don't believe you!"

The other fellow reached in his pocket, pulled out a sheet of paper and exclaimed, "Don't believe me? Here's the cancellation!"

. . . .

Two grocery advertising agency executives were having lunch when one exclaimed, "Oh, by the way, did you hear Herman Foofnik passed away yesterday?" The other executive gasped, "Oh, I'm sorry to hear that. He was such a nice fellow. What did he have?"

"Oh, nothing much," the other fellow sighed, "A small grocery account."

. . . .

Two men met at a cocktail party. The first fellow introduced himself and asked, "And what line of business are you in, sir?" The second gentleman replied, "I'm in cloaks and suits. Have you ever heard of the firm of Cohen and Murphy?"

The first gentleman smiled and said, "Oh, of course. But

a firm by the name of Cohen and Murphy, my, isn't that surprising!"

The second fellow smiled and added, "I got another surprise for you...I'm Murphy!"

. . . .

Two old timers happened to meet on the street. "*Nu* — Sam, I haven't see you since we left the old country. So how's business?" The second old timer smiled, "Couldn't be better — business is booming!"

"Aha!" exclaimed the first fellow, "In that case, could you loan me $5?"

"What, me loan you $5?" shouted the second old timer, "Why, I hardly know you!"

The first old timer sighed sadly, "I don't understand this world — in the old country, no one would loan me any money because they *knew* me, and here in America they won't lend me any money because they *don't* know me!"

. . . .

Two old timers went out to play golf. As they were getting ready to tee off, one of the players said, "Sam, I just noticed that you have only one golf ball. Don't you think you should have at least another, just in case you lose this one?"

Sam smiled and said, "I don't need any other balls. I can't lose this one. This is a very special ball!"

"Oh yeah," said the first fellow. "What if you hit the ball into the lake?"

Sam smiled once more, "No problem. This ball floats. So I'd be able to retrieve it in a second."

"Okay," the first fellow exclaimed, "But what if you hit the ball into the woods with all the bushes and trees. How will you be able to find it?"

"This ball has a homing device in it and gives off a beep. I can pick up the sound and retrieve the ball in no time."

"That's great," the first fellow said, "But what if the game runs late and it gets dark and you hit into a sand trap? What are you going to do then?"

Sam smiled once more, "No problem! This ball is fluorescent and lights up in the dark."

"That is truly an amazing ball," the first fellow exclaimed. "Where did you get it?"

Sam, smiled, "Oh, I found it!"

. . . .

Two old timers were sitting on a subway during the late evening hours. Suddenly, the train stopped, and a gang of hoods got on. One pulled out a weapon and announced, "This is a stick up!" and began going down the train grabbing the wallets of each passenger.

One of the old timers pulled a $20 bill out of his pocket and turned to his friend, "Chaim, here's the $20 I owe you."

Two partners in the Garment Center trusted each other implicitly. One day, one of the partners got the flu and had to stay home. A little later in the afternoon, the other partner called.

"Sam, I just opened the safe and discovered there's $5,000 missing. What should I do?"

"Put it back!" snapped the sick one.

. . . .

Two partners finished reviewing their business ledger together. "We must be thankful for everything," commented Sam.

"Thankful?" screeched his partner. "Look at these bills! We're going into bankruptcy! What have we got to be thankful for?"

The first fellow smiled and said, "We have to be thankful we're not one of our creditors!"

. . . .

When Cohen came to America, he struggled mightily to earn a living. One day, he called in his partner Moishe. "If we hit $1 million by the time my son Irving is ready for his Bar Mitzvah, I'll make him a celebration the likes of which the world has never seen and will never see again!"

"*Nu*, what would you do that would be so different?"

Sam thought for a moment and said, "Well, first I would hire out the Queen Elizabeth ocean liner, and then I would send invitations to my family and friends and all my clients.

Then, I would tell the captain to aim the boat toward Africa. Then, when we land in Africa, we'll make up a safari, and, on elephants we will march into the heart of the jungle, and there in G-d's wilderness, I will make my son's Bar Mitzvah."

And so, the good L-rd smiled upon them and they made millions. And true to his word, Sam hired out the Queen Elizabeth and loaded the ship with friends and relatives. Not a cent was spared.

The ship raced toward the coast of Africa. And just like Sam said, at the dock, an elephant safari was waiting. The 3,000 guests got off the ship and mounted the thousands of elephants.

The lead elephant driver lined them up in rows of two and began to move toward the jungle. Sam rode next to the lead elephant driver, as they plodded along the road.

After they had gone about two miles, the elephant driver called back, "Listen up, everyone! From this point on we must travel in single file." The elephants began to maneuver into position.

A little indignant that his guests had to be inconvenienced, Sam asked the elephant driver, "Say, listen, why do we have to go single file?"

"Because," began the elephant driver, "We have to clear part of the road to make room for the other Bar Mitzvah group coming back!"

Law & Order

. . . .

A fellow goes to a real hot-shot lawyer for advice. "My friend," exclaimed the lawyer, "$250 entitles you to ask three questions."

The fellow asks, "Well, what kind of questions do you want me to ask?"

The lawyer replies, "You may ask questions about anything you feel is important."

The young man says, "Well, isn't $250 an awful lot to charge for just three questions?"

The attorney smiles and says, "That's true. Now, what is your third question?"

A fellow walks into a bar and shouts, "All lawyers are idiots!"

A fellow responds, "I resent that remark!"

The first guy says, "Are you a lawyer?"

"No, I'm an idiot!" came the retort.

. . . .

A friend of mine, who is an attorney, went to a judge and told him that his client, for whom he had just won a case, refused to pay his fee.

"Did you present your request in writing?" asked the judge.

"Yes, l did," replied the attorney.

"And what did he say?" asked the judge.

"He told me to go to the devil."

"Then what did you do?" asked the judge.

"I came straight to you, sir!" exclaimed the attorney.

. . . .

A group of eggheads, riding on a bus, began discussing bible history. They were talking about which profession was first established following creation.

"It must have been a lawyer," exclaimed one man in a Homburg hat. "Man could never have survived the first days of creation if he didn't have laws to govern himself!"

"Laws?" scoffed the second man, "Cain and Abel couldn't have been born if there hadn't been a doctor around!"

"You're both wrong," exclaimed an architect. "Before Adam and Eve, there had to be an architect around to bring some order out of the chaos!"

"Aha, gentlemen!" chortled the man with the Homburg hat, "And who do you think created all the chaos?"

. . . .

A law professor was explaining courtroom procedure to his students. "Remember, when you are fighting a case, if you have the facts on your side, hammer on the facts! If you have the law on your side, hammer on the law."

A student raised his hand and asked, "But what if you don't have the facts, or the law, on your side?"

"In that case, you hammer on the table!"

. . . .

A lawyer came running into the courtroom after his client had been found guilty of a crime. He shouted to the judge, "Your honor, I demand that my client be given a new trial. I have just uncovered new evidence!"

The judge raised an eyebrow and said, "Well, that shouldn't be a problem. What is the new evidence that should warrant a new trial?"

The young lawyer took a deep breath and declared, "My

client has an extra $2,000 in his name that I can still bill him for, and I just found out about it this morning!"

⸱ ⸱

A lawyer was riding on a bus when he overheard two businessmen talking. Said one to the other, "I'll tell you about the law profession — lawyers are just people who help you get what's coming to them!"

⸱ ⸱

A motorcycle cop was hiding on the side of the highway, looking for speeders, when along came a car going just twenty-two miles per hour. Going so slow is just as dangerous as speeding. So, the cop turned on his lights and siren and pulled the car over.

As he approached the car, he noticed that there were five old ladies seated in the car. Two were seated in the front seat and three in the back. Four of the ladies were as white as ghosts and their eyes were wide open as if they were in shock.

"I wasn't speeding," the sweet little old lady, who was driving, said.

"I know that Ma'am," the officer said. "You should know that driving slower than the speed limit is a danger to other drivers."

"Slower than the speed limit? I was not!" she said. "I was driving at exactly twenty-two miles per hour, just like the speed limit says on those signs along the road!"

The cop started to laugh and explained that the twenty-two was the route number, not the speed limit.

A bit embarrassed, the woman grinned and thanked the officer.

"But before I let you go," he said. "Is everyone in the car okay? These women in the back are as white as ghosts. They look a bit shaken and haven't muttered a sound since I stopped you."

"Oh, they'll be okay in a minute. You see, we just got off route 119."

· ·

A speeding driver was signaled to the side of the highway by a motorcycle officer. "I want you to know that I am a very good friend of the Mayor," pleaded the speeder.

"Great," said the officer, as he wrote the ticket. "Now he'll know I'm on the job."

· ·

A store on the Lower East Side was constantly getting broken into. Finally, the owner made a little engraved sign that he placed on his door. It read, "NOTICE TO THIEVES! THIS STORE HAS BEEN ROBBED FIVE TIMES. MY TYPEWRITER IS GONE, AND SO IS MY ADDING-MACHINE. THE CASH REGISTER WAS STOLEN THE FIRST TIME, SO NO MONEY IS KEPT IN THE STORE. THERE IS NOTHING OF VALUE LEFT IN THE STORE."

The following day, when he came to open the store, he discovered someone had stolen his beautiful engraved sign.

- -

A traffic cop stopped a politician who was speeding. "Now wait a minute officer," the politician explained. "Do you realize that I'm a personal friend of Mayor Dinkins? I'm a close friend of Andrew Stein, and District Attorney Charles Hynes is a real close, personal friend."

The police officer asked, "Well, do you know Hymie Rabinowitz?"

"Who's he?" ask the politician.

Handing the politician a traffic ticket, he replied, "Me!"

- -

A woman and her little girl were visiting the grave of the little girl's grandmother. On their way through the cemetery and back to the car, the little girl asked, "Mommy, do they ever bury two people in the same grave?"

"Of course not, dear," replied the mother, "Why would you ask?"

"Well, the tombstone back there says, 'Herein lies a lawyer and an honest man!'"

- -

A woman appearing before a judge exclaimed, "Your Honor, my boss yells at me and gives me unlimited heartache. In fact, I lost twenty pounds from aggravation alone!"

The judge said, "By all means, I can force him to pay you severance and find you another job immediately!"

The woman reconsidered, "Please wait a couple more weeks, I need to lose another fifteen pounds!"

• •

A young boy walked up to his father and asked, "Dad, does a lawyer ever tell the truth?"

The father thought for a moment. "Yes, son," he replied. "A lawyer will do anything to win a case."

• •

A young lady went to her lawyer, who said he would only take a contingent fee.

"Excuse me," she asked, "What is a contingent fee?"

The lawyer smiled, "Well, if we don't win, I get nothing. If we do win, then you get nothing."

• •

A young man checked into a hotel and handed the desk clerk $500 to place in the hotel safe. The next morning, he went to the clerk and asked for his money.

"I don't know what you're talking about," exclaimed the clerk. "Do you have a receipt for that money?"

"Well, no," explained the young man.

"I'm sorry. You must be mistaken," said the clerk.

The young man went to a lawyer and told him what happened. The lawyer said, "Take another $500 and bring it to the clerk; only this time, have a friend with you. Then, about an hour later, return, without your friend, and ask for the money. This time the clerk will return the money because he knows you had a witness. Then, two hours later, come back to the clerk with your friend and ask the clerk for your money. The clerk will feel trapped and give you back the first $500 he took from you."

The young man did just what he was told and sure enough got all his money back. When he went to thank the lawyer, he asked.

"What do I owe you?"

The lawyer replied. "$500!"

. . . .

After twenty years, Mr. Foofnik hired an attorney to help dissolve his business partnership and to get the best deal. One day, the attorney called and exclaimed, "Well, Mr. Foofnik, when I took this case, I told you I would try to avoid a lengthy court litigation, and so I did — I worked out an out-of-court settlement with your partner that I believe is eminently fair to both of you!"

"Fair to both of us!" he screamed, "Listen, for that I had to hire a lawyer? I could have done that myself!"

An angel from heaven was having a dispute with one of Satan's angels. It seems that the gate separating heaven from the other place down below was broken. The angel from heaven called up the angel from down there and said, "Listen, the front gate separating our domains is broken. The last time it broke we fixed it, and you signed an agreement that your men would fix it if it ever broke again."

Satan's angel grumbled, "Will you stop bugging us? My men are too busy tending to the fires down here. I can't take them off their job just to fix a gate!"

The angel from heaven said, "Okay, have it your way. We'll just have to sue you for breaking our agreement."

And the angel from the fiery place down below sneered, "Oh yeah? Where ya gonna find a lawyer?"

• •

An old timer who had just one too many drinks was weaving all over the road and kept crossing over the line of arrows that separated the roadway. Finally, he was pulled over by a cop, who shouted, "Are you crazy or something? Didn't you see the arrows?"

The old timer shrugged, "I didn't even see the Indians!"

• •

An old timer, who was prone to exaggerating, was driving on the Belt Parkway in Brooklyn, when he was flagged down by a cop for exceeding the 50 miles per hour speeding limit.

"What do mean I was going 60?" the old timer exclaimed. "I wasn't even doing 50! In fact, I wasn't even going 30. I don't think I was doing 10 miles an hour! In fact, couldn't you see I was parked?"

The cop nodded and promptly gave him a ticket for parking on a public highway.

. . . .

Cohen had been a victim of a bus accident and a jury had just awarded him more than $100,000. His jubilation ended when the attorney reminded him, "You know, I get 70% of that settlement."

Cohen shouted, "You're a *gonif!* You forget I was the one knocked down by the bus and dragged two blocks!"

"You're absolutely right," the attorney replied. "However, you have to recognize the fact that it was my legal know-how and my persuasion that won the case for you and got the jury to give you the award. Any idiot could get knocked down by a bus and be dragged two blocks!"

. . . .

Cohen had received a shipment of merchandise that had been damaged in transit, and he refused to pay. As a result, he was sued. He hired a lawyer and went to court. Halfway through the trial, Cohen had to leave the city to visit an out of town client on a big deal.

"But, remember," he ordered his attorney, "The minute the case is over, send me a telegram on how we made out!" The attorney promised he'd send the telegram and went back to court.

A few days later, by some quirk of fate, the case was settled in Cohen's favor. The attorney ran to a Western Union office and telegrammed Cohen, "Right has triumphed! Justice has been proven!"

Cohen wired back, "Appeal immediately!"

· ·

Cohen had some legal matters with his attorney and when the matters were resolved, he got a bill from his attorney that made him swoon. When he called his lawyer, the lawyer explained, "Listen, time is my stock-and-trade. Whenever you'd call me to ask a question, I'd mark it down, and based on the amount of time I spoke with you, that is how much I charged you."

There was little Cohen could do but pay the bill. A few days later, while going out for lunch, he met his lawyer on the street.

"Nice day isn't it?" Cohen exclaimed, then quickly realizing he was asking a question, snapped, "I'm *telling* you, not *asking!*"

· ·

Cohen was at a small resort and wanted to consult with an attorney concerning a theft at his place of business.

He approached the local police chief and asked, "Excuse me, but do you have a criminal lawyer in these parts?"

The police chief thought for a moment, then exclaimed, "Yes we do, but we can't exactly get the goods on him!"

• •

Cohen was barreling down the Belt Parkway in Brooklyn when a motorcycle cop hailed him to the side of the road.

"You were speeding and I'm going to give you a ticket for doing 60 miles per hour in a 50 mile per hour zone."

Cohen thought for a minute, then turned to the officer and pleaded, "Could you make that read '75 miles per hour in a 50 miles per hour zone' — you see, I'm trying to sell the car!"

• •

Cohen was suing Rabinowitz. At lunch, Cohen told his lawyer, "I just sent a box of cigars to the judge." The lawyer gasped, "Mr. Cohen — are you crazy — that will look like you are trying to bribe the judge!"

"I know," sighed Cohen, "That's why I signed Rabinowitz's name!"

• •

Goldberg went to a lawyer to straighten out some legal problems. The attorney asked a number of questions and spent more than four hours with the client. A few days later, the attorney sent Goldberg a *Geshvolener* (extremely high) bill for his services.

Goldberg called the attorney and asked, "Say, what is this bill for?"

The attorney explained, "For the questions I asked you, remember? With the information I obtained from you, we won our case."

"But how did you arrive at such a figure?" pleaded Goldberg.

"Well, if you must know," the attorney explained, nearly exasperated, "Figure it out this way. I asked you 200 questions and I figure $10 a question, so my fee is $2,000."

Goldberg could not help himself and sent a check. Later, the lawyer came by.

"How are you?" he asked.

Goldberg didn't say a word but merely shrugged to a passerby, "At $10 a question, it's his business?"

. . . .

Heard in Family Court:

"Well, sir," announced the Judge, "I have reviewed this case and I have decided to give your wife $500 a week."

"That's nice, your Honor," the husband replied. "I'll try to send her a few bucks myself every now and then."

. . . .

Irving Kuchleffel was standing on the corner of Eastern Parkway and Franklin Avenue, when a car went out of control and hit two other cars parked in the area. A police officer arrived at the scene, and Kuchleffel's name was taken as a witness. In a few weeks, he was called to court to testify.

"Mr. Kuchleffel," the attorney began, "would you please tell the court, on the date in question, did you see an accident?"

Kuchleffel beamed proudly with his sudden importance. "Did I see an accident? How could I have missed it? Wasn't I there? Didn't the policeman tell you?"

The attorney smiled weakly, "Err, Mr. Kuchleffel, were you standing on the corner at the time?"

Kuchleffel straightened up proudly and declared, "Where else was I standing, in a tree?"

The attorney tried once more, "Since you saw the accident from its very inception, would you say it was the fault of the defendant?"

Kuchleffel lifted his brow, "Whose fault was it? Maybe it was my fault?"

The judge was becoming angrier and angrier. Finally, he turned to Kuchleffel, "Mr. Kuchleffel, can't you answer a question without asking another question?"

Kuchleffel looked up indignantly, "Sure, why not?"

. . . .

Irving was in court for the first time as a witness. He was sworn in and then the judge turned to him and asked, "Tell me, do you know what will happen if you don't tell the truth?" Irving nodded, "Yes, your Honor, our side will win!"

It seems an attorney was severely badgering a defendant on the stand.

"Tell me," exclaimed the attorney, "You say you slightly pushed the complainant."

"That's right," admitted the defendant.

"Would you please step off the stand and demonstrate what you call 'slightly' pushing?" the district attorney sneered.

The defendant realized that if he demonstrated too severely he would seal his doom, but he couldn't let the aggressive attorney get away with the badgering. So, the defendant stepped off the stand, went over to the attorney, and gave him a wallop on the jaw. He then punched and pummeled him mercilessly.

He then got back on the stand, turned to the Judge and said, "Your honor, I hit the complainant about one-tenth of that."

. . . .

It was a major criminal case. Cohen was called to the stand as a character witness for his partner, Lebowitz.

"Now tell me sir," asked the prosecution, "The defendant claims he was with you on the night in question. Can you tell the court where you were on the night of April 2nd?"

"I object," shouted the defense attorney.

Before the judge could even rule on the objection, Cohen shouted, "It's alright — I don't mind answering the question."

The prosecutor took a deep breath and once more asked, "Now, tell us sir, where were you on the night of April 2nd?"

"I object!" shouted the defense attorney once more.

"It's alright," shouted Cohen once more. "I can answer his question!"

The judge turned to the defense counsel and said, "Apparently the witness wants to answer the question. Go ahead, Mr. Cohen, you may answer the question."

"Now, tell me, where were you on the night of April 2nd?"

Cohen shrugged his shoulders with all innocence and replied, "Who knows?"

• •

Moishe, a garment manufacturer, calls up his attorney. "Charlie, listen, I have a situation I would like to explain to you, but I'm not going to pay you a cent unless you think there really is a cause of action."

The attorney says, "Go ahead,"

"Well," Moishe begins, "Some goods were sold and received, but they were full of holes and all kinds of damages. Should the bill be paid?"

The attorney commented, "Are you kidding, that's a perfect cause of action. It will cost you $250 for me to start an action. Should I start?"

Louie sighed, "No, never mind, I was telling you the other fellow's side of the story!"

My mother is a typical Jewish mother. Once, she was on jury duty. They sent her home because she insisted *she* was guilty!

• •

Myron Rabinowitz was the complainant in an accident case. When it came his turn to be put on the witness stand, he started to shake nervously.

In an effort to restore his confidence, his attorney stepped forward and whispered in his ear, "Myron, you have nothing to worry about. Just answer the questions truthfully. Tell them, in my own words, exactly how it happened!"

• •

One afternoon, Cohen met his lawyer in the elevator and casually said, "You know, it looks like rain. Do you think I need an umbrella?"

The lawyer smiled and said, "No, I don't think so."

The following day, the lawyer sent Cohen a bill for $50 for "advice."

The next day, he met the lawyer in the elevator and commented, "It's nice to meet you again. What floor are you coming from?"

The lawyer smiled and said, "The 15th!"

The following day, Cohen got a bill for $35 for "information."

The next day Cohen met his lawyer in the elevator. He

turned to him and exclaimed. "Do you know there are some no-good chiselers in this world who call themselves lawyers. And remember, this time I'm telling you — not asking!"

. . . .

Question: "Is your appearance here this morning pursuant to a deposition that I sent to your attorney?"

Answer: "No, this is how I normally dress."

. . . .

Sadie Nuchamol came before a judge and declared, "I was attacked!"

"When did this happen?" asked the judge.

"About thirty-five years ago."

"So how come you're complaining now?" asked the Judge.

"Who's complaining? I came to reminisce!"

. . . .

Sadie Rabinowitz was called as a witness in a trial involving an accident that took place in front of her neighbor's house. She was put on the stand and questioned by the attorney. "Mrs. Rabinowitz, could you please tell the court what happened to you on May 30th of this year?"

At that moment, the defense attorney jumped to his feet and shouted, "I object, your Honor, I object!"

The judge said, "Objection overruled! The woman is a

witness in this matter and is allowed to tell what happened to her on May 30th. Go ahead Mrs. Rabinowitz..."

"Well, on May 30th I went out to hang out my laundry to dry. Then I walked over to Mrs. Cohen, my neighbor's house, and rang the doorbell."

The defense attorney was up on his feet once more. "I object your Honor! I object! Mrs. Cohen, the next-door neighbor, admitted not seeing the accident, so how could we accept testimony from this woman who went to visit with Mrs. Cohen?"

It was a hassle never before seen in the court. Both sides argued for almost an hour. Finally, the judge said, "I must overrule the objection!"

The attorney turned back to Mrs. Rabinowitz and repeated, "Okay, now tell us, what did Mrs. Cohen say after you rang her bell."

Mrs. Rabinowitz smiled sheepishly and exclaimed, "Nothing, she wasn't home!"

⋯⋯⋯⋯⋯⋯⋯⋯⋯⋯⋯⋯⋯⋯⋯

Sadie's husband was injured in an automobile accident. A few months later, her friend called up and asked, "*Nu*, so how is Sam? Can he walk yet?"

Sadie replied, "Well, that depends — the doctor says he can, but the lawyer says he can't!"

Several women, each trying to one-up the other, appeared in court, each accusing the other of causing the trouble they were having in the apartment building where they lived.

The judge, with Solomon-like wisdom, decreed, "Okay, I'm ready to hear the evidence. I'll hear the oldest first."

The case was promptly dismissed for lack of testimony.

* *

Shloimy was called for jury duty. When he was put on the witness stand to be interviewed, he turned to the judge and said, "Your honor, I can't serve on the jury — why, one look at that guy and I'm convinced he's guilty!"

"Excused," snapped the judge, "That's the District Attorney!"

* *

Shloimy was suing the city and was testifying on the witness stand. "I was walking on the sidewalk when I fell in a hole."

The judge asked, "Were you walking east or west?"

The man repeated, "I was walking on the sidewalk when I fell into a hole."

The judge interjected, "Sir, were you walking toward the drive or away from it?"

The man repeated once more, "I was walking on the sidewalk when I fell into a hole."

The judge shouted, "Why do you keep avoiding my question?"

The man replied, "Because if I move one inch from the hole in the sidewalk, I lose my case."

. . . .

The burglar alarm went off in the jewelry store, and in minutes, the police had Sam in custody. When he was brought before the Judge, he was asked, "Did you have an accomplice on that job?"

Sam asked, "What's an accomplice?"

The judge explained, "That's a partner. In other words, did you commit the crime by yourself?"

Sam smiled sadly as he stood between the two huge cops and exclaimed, "What else? Who can get reliable help these days?"

. . . .

The cashier of a local restaurant took off with a large sum of money. When the detective came in, he asked the boss for a description. "Tell me, Mr. Cohen, was he tall or short?"

Cohen sighed, "Both!"

. . . .

The defendant in a large fraud and theft case was having difficulty getting a lawyer to defend him.

The judge asked, "Why can't you get a lawyer to defend yourself?"

The defendant said, "As soon as they found out I didn't steal all the money I'm accused of taking, they all quit!"

. . . .

The judge was furious when the jury notified him that they could not reach a verdict. The judge called the jury into the courtroom and began to berate them.

"You ought to be ashamed of yourselves. You did not pay close attention. You failed to grasp the legal fundamentals!"

Goldberg, a sweet little old timer on the jury, raised his hand and declared, "Please, Judge — don't be mad at us, we all agree with you!"

. . . .

The legal profession has always been known to be the ultimate in reserved gentlemanly distinction. So, it came as rather a jolt when Cohen's lawyer got up in court and shouted to Shapiro's lawyer, "You are a cheap, no-good crook, a phony nincompoop, and an ambulance-chaser!"

Shapiro's lawyer shot back, "And you, my friend, are a cheap shyster of the worst order. You are a corrupt fool and a dope!"

At that moment the judge shouted, "Gentlemen, please! Now let's proceed with the case since both learned counsels have identified themselves!"

The police officer hailed the car to the curb. "Alright, what's the big hurry?" the officer exclaimed.

"I'm late for an appointment …" the driver tried to explain.

"Oh yeah, what's your name?" the officer demanded.

"Shlomo Ben Zaddick Affremchilneekidov," the motorist said.

The officer put his book away, cleared his throat and said, "Well, don't let me catch you again!"

. . . .

Two lawyers talking to each other. "Gee, I flunked the Bar again. And I was so close to the right answers!"

The friend asks, "How close were you?"

The first lawyer sighs, "About three seats away!"

. . . .

Two proud grandmothers were sitting on a porch in the mountains. "My grandson is a lawyer," she exclaimed to the lady sitting next to her.

"Is that so?" the lady commented. "So, how's he doing?"

The first grandmother replied, "This boy is so brilliant, he could look at a contract and immediately tell you whether it's oral or written!"

Velvel and Moishe had some business dealings with a lawyer. When they got their bill it read, "For services rendered June 14; ditto June 18; ditto June 22; ditto June 28."

Each partner looked at the bill and couldn't understand it. They figured if they had to call a lawyer to find out what 'ditto' stood for, he'd bill them for the information. So instead, Velvel ran to the library and spent hours researching the word 'ditto.'

At the end of the day, he returned to his shop. His partner questioned, "*Nu* Velvel, did you find out what this 'ditto' business is?"

"Yes, I did!" exclaimed Sam, "I found out that I'm Velvel and you're ditto!"

· ·

Watching a trial in court, one spectator whispered to another, "Justice is blind!"

"You can talk louder, it is deaf, too!" came the reply.

Food & Dining

· ·

A customer entered a small grocery store and said to the man behind the counter, "A dozen eggs, please."

The grocer inquired, "We have 1st grade eggs, 2nd grade eggs and 3rd grade eggs. Which grade would you like?"

The customer countered, "Just let me have some that have already graduated."

· ·

A fellow called up his friend and said, "Hello Sam? I heard you bought a restaurant."

"That's right," Sam replied.

"And I also heard when there was a power failure, your

refrigeration went out, and you lost everything that was in your freezer."

"That's true," sighed Sam.

"And I also heard that because of that, the Board of Health had to close you down, and you had to borrow $5,000 from the bank to get started again."

"That's true," Sam replied.

"And now you're back in business."

"*Nu*, so you already had all the information," Sam said with annoyance.

"Sure," replied the caller, "But this is the first time I'm hearing all the details!"

. . . .

A fellow is in a lunchroom and shouts out, "Waiter! This coffee tastes like mud."

The waiter says, "Yes sir — it's freshly ground!"

. . . .

A fellow walked into a small restaurant and ordered a steak. The waiter brought him a tremendous steak with all the trimmings. The following day, he went back to the same restaurant and ordered another steak. This time the steak arrived and was half the size of the one served the day before. He called the manager over and said, "How come such a small steak today? Yesterday, the one you gave me was twice the size. How come?"

The manager smiled warmly and explained, "Yesterday you were sitting near the front window!"

. . . .

A new dairy restaurant opened in a local community. Cohen went in to try out the food. The following day, he was met by his friend.

"*Nu*, Cohen," the friend asked, "How was the new restaurant?"

Cohen sighed, "Terrible. The food was real poison — and such small portions!"

. . . .

A prominent singer once complained to a diner at an event that he seemed more preoccupied with his meal than with the entertainment.

"I'm sorry," the diner replied, "But I've seen singers before. This is the first time I've seen a $50 steak!"

. . . .

A restaurant owner sighed, "When I have food left over, I make hash. But my problem is, when I have hash left over, what do I make?"

A youngster is rebelling against eating a vegetable he does not like, so his mother tries to console him. "Eat your spinach dear, it makes strong teeth."

"Then why don't you feed it to grandpa?"

. . . .

An anti-Semitic Texan walked into a Chinese restaurant on the Lower East Side and snapped boisterously, "Got any new Jews in here?"

The little Chinese waiter smiled and said, "One moment, sir," and he walked into the kitchen. In a few minutes, he returned and smiled warmly.

"Sorry, sir — we have no new Jews, we only got orange Jews and pineapple Jews!"

. . . .

An old timer walked into a restaurant and ordered a bowl of soup. The waiter brought the soup and as the customer started to eat, he saw something swimming around in the soup. He called the waiter over and very discreetly asked, "What's this floating around in my soup?"

The waiter looked into the bowl, very concerned, and said, "Wait, I'll call my son at Columbia, he's an entomologist. I can't tell one insect from the other!"

An old timer opened a little refreshment stand on Coney Island, just off the boardwalk. But the old timer, in order to earn a little more profit, would add a little water to the syrups he used to make drinks. One day, an inspector passed by and bought a drink.

"Say, these drinks are diluted. You can't do that. There's a law that says you must post a sign about the ingredients of your drink."

"What difference does it make?" the old timer argued, "The customers don't complain."

"It makes no difference," the inspector argued, "You have to post a sign that you are adulterating your drinks with water!"

The following day, the old timer put up a sign and a few weeks later, the inspector passed by.

"Well, how's business?" he asked, caustically.

The old timer was all smiles, "You're a wonderful planner. Ever since you told me to put up the sign, my business has doubled!"

The inspector stepped back and read the sign. It said, "Every drink sold here is guaranteed to be highly adulterated with 100% pure H_2O."

．．．．．．．．．．．．．．．．．．．．．．．．．．．．．．．．．．．．

Cohen got himself a job in a fancy restaurant on the East Side. One day, a customer came in and ordered a bowl of soup. Sure enough, when the soup was brought out, the customer motioned to Cohen and exclaimed, "Listen, I don't want to make a scene, but there's a fly in my soup."

Cohen looked over, verified that there was, indeed, a fly in his soup, then he turned to the customer and exclaimed, "Congratulations! All day long the cook, the owner, and myself have been trying to catch that fly, and just imagine you, a total stranger, succeeded!"

. . . .

Cohen opened a new restaurant and was determined to cater to the community's needs. As he opened his doors, Izzy Goldberg came walking down the street and was greeted by Cohen, who seated him at his best table. Cohen filled Goldberg's plate to the point of almost overflowing. After Goldberg had finished eating, Cohen approached him.

"*Nu*, Goldberg, everything was okay?"

Goldberg scowled and commented, "The food was nice, but what's the idea of giving only two slices of bread?"

Cohen smiled apologetically and said, "Well, we just opened and don't know what the customers really want. If you'll stop in tomorrow, I'll see to it that there is plenty of bread."

The following day, when Cohen saw Goldberg walking down the street, he ran inside his restaurant and filled the breadbasket with 8 slices of bread.

"That ought to keep him happy," he thought to himself.

Goldberg sat down and finished every morsel, including the bread. As he left, Cohen smiled warmly, "*Nu*, so everything today was okay? Plenty of bread? Yes?"

Goldberg scowled and commented, "The food was okay, but what's the idea of giving only eight slices of bread — this I'm using when I'm on a diet!"

Cohen apologized and said, "Come in tomorrow and I'll see to it that you are satisfied."

The following day, as Goldberg came walking down the street, Cohen ran inside and took a 2-ft. long French bread and cut it down the middle. He placed this on the bread plate and smiled to himself, "I'd like to see him complain today!"

Goldberg came in and finished every crumb on the table. Cohen stood at the door with a smile from ear to ear and commented, "*Nu*, Goldberg — everything was good? Plenty of bread?"

Goldberg scowled as usual and commented wryly, "The food was good, like always, but what's the idea of going back to two slices of bread?"

. . . .

Cohen walked into a rather dumpy looking restaurant and noticed that the waiter looked familiar to him.

"Hey, excuse me, but didn't we go to college together?"

The waiter nodded, "Yes, we did."

"And weren't you the one who scored the highest marks on all the tests?"

The waiter nodded affirmatively again.

"And weren't you voted the most likely to succeed?"

The waiter nodded once more.

"Then tell me," Cohen asked, "What are you doing in a dumpy restaurant like this?"

The waiter sighed, "Listen, I don't eat here. But what's your excuse?"

. . . .

Cohen walked into a restaurant on the Lower East Side and ordered dinner. In a few minutes, the waiter brought his order. The chicken was like shoe-leather. The carrots and peas were cold and raw.

He pushed the plate aside and called the waiter. "This is terrible. I won't eat this! Call the manager!"

The waiter smiled meekly and said, "It wouldn't do any good, he wouldn't eat it either!"

. . . .

Cohen, who was down on his luck, walked into a restaurant and said to the owner, "I'll give you twice the cost of the meal if you can guess what I am!"

The owner, a betting man, asked, "How many guesses will I be permitted?"

"Unlimited" explained Cohen.

"That's a deal!" the owner exclaimed.

The man then wrote down what he was on a slip of paper and put it in a sealed envelope. The owner then began to guess. "Are you a baker, a butcher, an accountant..." He guessed for nearly 100 times and then finally gave up.

"Okay, what are you?"

The man handed the envelope to the owner, who promptly opened it.

Inside was written, "I am hungry!"

. . . .

Feivel owned a delicatessen but had a reputation for having a terrible disposition. He would start shouting at his customers for the slightest thing. Sure enough, a young Israeli walked into the store one day and went up to Feivel.

"Listen, I'll bet you $5 I can bite my own eye!"

Feivel looked at him and wanted to throw him out — but he was curious.

"Okay, you're on." He put $5 on the counter and the young Israeli covered the bet. Then he put his hand to his eye and removed a glass eye and began biting it. Then he picked up the money and smiled.

Feivel was furious and wanted to throw him out.

"Wait a minute," the Israeli said, "I'll give you a chance to get even. I'll bet you $10 that I can bite my other eye."

Feivel thought for a moment. Surely this he could not do. Two glass eyes he certainly didn't have. So he said, "Okay! It's a bet."

He put $10 on the counter and waited.

The young Israeli then put his hand to his mouth, took out a set of false teeth and put the teeth next to his other eye and began clicking away.

Feivel was more furious than ever and was ready to throw him out.

"Wait a minute, I'll give you a chance to make some real money. I'll bet you $100 that I can take a bottle of soda, shake it up, aim it at that little Schnapps glass at the end of counter and get every drop of soda out of the bottle into the Schnapps glass without getting a drop on the counter."

Now this had to be impossible, Feivel thought. How could he get a shaken-up bottle of soda into a Schnapps glass from 15-feet away? Absolutely impossible, even if it were a trick. "Okay!" said Feivel, putting $100 on the counter.

The young man took a bottle of soda and shook it violently. Then he snapped the cap off and the soda spurted all over the place! There wasn't a dry spot in the store. As a matter of fact, not even a drop got in the Schnapps glass.

Feivel began to laugh with joy, as he picked up the $100. Then, still roaring with laughter, he looked at the young man and asked, "Listen, I don't understand. It is absolutely impossible to shake up a bottle of soda and get it into a glass. Why did you make such a bet?"

The young Israeli smiled, "You see those two customers of yours sitting at that table? They told me you had the world's worst disposition. So, I bet them $400 that I could spray your whole place with soda and you wouldn't even get mad! In fact, I even bet them an extra $400 that you would be laughing!"

For the past 25 years, Cohen would eat in the very same restaurant on the Lower East Side. He was a model customer. However, one evening, he walked into the restaurant and ordered a bowl of borscht. The waiter brought the borscht. As he started to walk away, Cohen shouted after him, "Hey waiter, come here."

The waiter came back to his table. "Yes sir?"

"Taste this borscht!" Cohen said softly.

The waiter leaned over and said, "What's the matter with it?"

"Listen, just taste it," Cohen said a little louder.

"What's the matter, is it too cold, maybe?" the waiter asked softly.

"Taste this borscht!" Cohen shouted more indignantly.

"Listen if you don't want the borscht I'll take it back, what would you like instead?"

"TASTE THIS BORSCHT!" shouted Cohen in anger.

The waiter, intimidated by the shouting, said, "Okay — if you insist..." He then began looking around for a spoon.

"Err, where's the spoon?" he asked.

"Ah-ha!" exploded the customer.

• •

Goldberg and Lapidus went into a restaurant to order coffee. "And make sure my cup is clean," snapped Goldberg to the waitress.

She nodded and went to the counter for their coffees. In a few minutes, she returned with the coffee and asked, "Here's your coffee. Now, which one of you asked for the clean cup?"

. . . .

Goldberg was hungry and found himself out of money as he passed a knish place in Coney Island. He walked over to the proprietor and exclaimed, "Do you know I'm a champion knish eater — the greatest in the world! I can eat fifty knishes in fifteen minutes."

The owner looked at him skeptically. "You're crazy! No man can eat fifty knishes in fifteen minutes."

Goldberg smiled and said, "I'll bet you a nickel just to prove you wrong."

"Okay," exclaimed the owner, and he began serving knishes by the plate-load. In fifteen minutes, Goldberg had only eaten ten.

"Aha!" screamed the owner, "See, you couldn't do it. You're a faker!"

Goldberg shrugged and said, "I guess I've lost my touch." He quietly put down his nickel and walked out the door, his stomach now filled to capacity.

. . . .

Goldberg was traveling on one of those fancy trains in Paris. When he went to the dining car for breakfast, the waiter approached, smiled pleasantly as he bowed, and said, "*Bon Appétit!*"

Goldberg nodded and replied, "Goldberg!" The waiter smiled back and brought him his breakfast.

When lunchtime came, he went back to the dining ear. The waiter approached, all smiles, and bowed again, saying, "*Bon Appétit!*"

Goldberg smiled back and replied, "Goldberg!"

Later on, he asked a conductor, "What does he mean when he says this '*Bon Appétit?*'"

The conductor replied, "It means 'hearty appetite.' It's sort of a greeting."

Goldberg thanked him and, as dinner time approached, he went to the dining car to show his waiter that he appreciated his good wishes. As the waiter approached, Goldberg stood up, bowed lightly and said, "*Bon Appétit!*"

The waiter returned the smile, clicked his heels together, and replied, "Goldberg!"

. . . .

It was mealtime, and Rosie asked Irving, "Would you like dinner?"

"Yes," said Irving. "What are my choices?"

"Yes or no," she replied.

Kelly and Fitzpatrick accidentally wandered into a kosher restaurant. Kelly, playing the part of a man of the world, sat down and, while waiting for the waiter to take their order, promptly smeared a piece of bread with the attractively colored horseradish on the table. He thought it was a new kind of jelly.

He took one bite and his eyes filled with tears. The horseradish was so strong. In an effort to cover up his mistake, he continued to eat the bread and horseradish with tears flowing profusely.

Fitzpatrick realizing something was askew asked, "And what bothers you my good friend? Eat something that doesn't agree with you?"

Kelly swallowed hard and exclaimed, "Of course not, I know all these foods, it's just that I was thinking about my dear old grandfather and the time he was hung."

"Why don't you try some of this kosher jelly?" Kelly asked, still keeping up the bluff.

Fitzpatrick smeared a slice of bread with the red-hot horseradish. He took one bite and his ears practically lit up. His eyes filled with tears. But he couldn't admit to Kelly that he had been taken.

"And what bothers you my old friend?" asked Kelly, trying to hold back his laughter.

Fitzpatrick cleared his throat and gasped, "I was just crying because I was thinking of your old grandfather and wondering why they didn't hang you at the same time?"

One hot summer's day a bum sauntered into a kosher restaurant and started to make preparations for a big meal. First, he removed his jacket, then he took off his collar and finally he began to roll up the sleeves of his shirt. The patrons of that eating place viewed his operations with loud merriment and the attention of the proprietor was soon aroused.

"Say, mister," shouted the restaurant man as he ran up to the person, "What do you think this is, a Turkish bath?"

"When I have my meal, I like to feel comfortable," declared the unconventional patron.

"What do you mean?" demanded the owner of the restaurant, "Would you do the same thing at the Victoria?"

"I do the same thing wherever I come," declared the manner-less man. "In fact, I am just coming from the Victoria, and there, too, I do the same things."

"And what did the proprietor say?" queried the restaurateur.

"He said if I wanted comfort, I'd better go to Solomon's Restaurant — so here I am!"

• •

Sam had made it rich in the stock market and decided to visit his old partner in the Garment Center. "Irving, today I am going to take you out for a dinner like you never had in your life. Money is no longer an object with me."

Irving put on his jacket and the two walked, arm in arm, to one of the fanciest rooftop restaurants overlooking Central

Park. As they sat down, Sam whispered, "I want you to know this is the only kosher, super-refined restaurant in all of New York City. I know the *Mashgiach* personally. When it's slow here, he plays the piano. Order whatever you want. Everything here is 100%."

The two ordered the fanciest dishes on the menu. The service was phenomenal, with four waiters at their side and fresh silverware for every dish. As they finished the meal, the waiters put down the fanciest little finger bowls you ever saw with little flowers and a flick of lemon floating on a boat of fresh orange.

"What's this?" Irving asked Sam.

"This I didn't order."

"We'll ask the waiter," Sam suggested as he motioned to the waiter.

"Pardon me," he said, "What do you call this?"

"That, sir," the waiter said coldly, "Is a finger bowl with *Eau de Vichy*. You use them to rinse your fingers."

Sam looked at Irving, shrugged innocently, then said, "*Nu…* you ask a silly question, you get a silly answer!"

. . . .

Shmuel opened a restaurant and lamented to his friend, "*Oy*, business is terrible. My corporate customers won't pay their bills."

"Don't worry," consoled his friend, "In this business, you'll always have customers who don't pay their bills."

Shmuel sighed, "I know, but now even the customers who don't pay their bills have stopped ordering!"

· ·

The old timer was nearly out of breath when he got home. "Chana, I've just been to the house of the richest man in our village and he was eating blintzes. Oh, my—what a delicacy! I stood in his house and those smells and juices went to work on me. *Gevald!* Were they delicious! Believe me, when rich people eat, they sure know how! I only wish that before I pass from this world, I could taste blintzes like a rich man! That's my only wish."

His wife smiled and said, "Yankel, if that's all it takes to make you happy, I'll make them for you. Oh, wait a minute — we don't have any eggs and we don't have enough money for eggs."

"*Nu,*" shrugged the old timer, "So make them without eggs."

"All right," agreed his wife, who then suddenly announced, "*Oy vey,* we don't have any cheese to fill them with."

"*Nu,* so we'll live without the cheese in the middle," the old timer suggested.

As his wife began once more, she discovered, "*Oy,* I didn't realize we don't have any sugar in the house, either."

"*Nu,* so we can live without sugar, also. Go make them already — I can hardly wait!"

In a few minutes, the wife, determined to please her husband, struggled with the little concoction, without eggs, cheese, or sugar, and tried to make blintzes. Indeed, an impossible task.

She placed the melting glob of butter on her husband's plate, and he began to eat.

Then a look of bewilderment crossed his face as he declared, "If I live to be a 100, I'll never understand what those rich people see in blintzes!"

. . . .

The waiters in some of the East Side restaurants are still magnificent. For example, last week I stopped in at one of the traditional old time eating places on the Lower East Side and ordered a cup of coffee. When the waiter brought the coffee, I commented, "Say, this coffee tastes terrible. It tastes like kerosene!"

The waiter turned politely and exclaimed, "If it tastes like kerosene, it must be tea, because the coffee tastes like turpentine!"

. . . .

Two little fellows walked into an ice cream store and asked for vanilla ice cream cones. The storekeeper was all out of vanilla and only had the strawberry flavor left. He promptly filled up the two cones, handed them to the little fellows and exclaimed, "Here you are — two pink vanilla ice cream specials!"

Parenting & Children

. . . .

A boy had been asking his father for money a little too frequently. His dad decided that it was time for a little lecture. At the end of his talk, he asked if his son realized how long and hard he worked to get the money he had. The son was silent and thoughtful for a moment, and answered, "You're lucky you can work for yours — I have to beg for mine!"

. . . .

A father was talking to his teenage son. "Do you realize when George Washington was your age, he was already a surveyor and was earning a fabulous salary?"

The son replied, "That's true. But did you realize, Dad, when George Washington was your age, he was already President of the United States?"

. . . .

A fellow called his credit card company and reported his card was stolen a month ago.

"Why didn't you report it immediately?" the clerk asked him.

The fellow cleared his throat and said, "Well, for one thing, the person who stole it was spending less than my kids did — so I felt I was ahead of the game."

. . . .

A fellow had a son who joined every club in town, wasting many hours in each. Finally, in desperation, the father went to the sage old rabbi and asked, "Rabbi, tell me, I need your advice. Do you believe in clubs for adolescent children?"

The old timer stroked his beard solemnly and declared, "Why, of course not! Never use hands in disciplining a child!"

. . . .

A fellow walked into a handbag store and said, "I'd like to get a purse for my wife." The girl smiled and said, "Is it going to be a surprise?" The old timer smiled back, "Sure is! She thinks she's getting a new car!"

A friend asked my wife, "What is your son taking in college?"

"All we got!" my wife sighed.

· ·

A friend of mine just had a new baby boy. One of the employees in his place wanted to place a huge sign over the doorway for all to see that his wife had given birth. But before he would put the sign up, he asked his partner for the inscription and the size of the sign. The partner wrote the information on a sheet of paper and left it on the switchboard operator's desk while she was out for lunch.

When she came back, she nearly fainted as she read the note. It read: "My wife had a boy — eight feet long and three feet wide!"

· ·

A grandmother was telling her little granddaughter what her own childhood was like. "We used to skate outside on a pond. I had a swing made from afar. We rode a pony. And we picked wild-blueberries in the woods."

The little girl listened, wide-eyed. Then she said, "Sure wish I had gotten to know you sooner!"

· ·

A lady and her little son were riding on a train. A woman sitting next to the little child offered him an apple. The mother smiled warmly and said to the little one, "Shloimy, what do you say to the nice lady?"

The child smiled and said, "Peel it!"

. . . .

A little boy who saw triplets for the first time in his life came running into the house exclaiming, "Mommy, Mommy, I just saw a lady that had twins and a spare!"

. . . .

A little kid came running into the house and shouted, "Ma, could I watch the solar eclipse?"

The mother replied, "Yes darling, but don't get too close."

. . . .

A nursery school teacher was explaining to her little wards the importance of being observant. "Aside from the *mezuzah* that we have on our doorposts, can you think of any other things in your house that are related to prayer?" the teacher asked.

The little ones thought, then one raised her hand and said brightly, "We have candlesticks that my mother puts candles in every Friday night."

Another youngster raised his hand and said, "My father puts on tefillin every morning."

The teacher nodded her approval.

And then another little one raised her hand and spoke hesitatingly. "We have something in my house, too, that must be a religious article, but I don't know what it is."

The teacher looked puzzled. "Well, could you describe it?"

The little one sighed, "Well, it's a flat thing with a little platform and has some numbers that move when you step on it. Every morning when my mommy steps on it and looks at the numbers, I think she prays, because she always says, 'Oh, heavens!'"

• •

A psychologist recently commented, "Kids who never come when they are called will probably grow up to be doctors; and kids who show up without being called probably will grow up to be lawyers."

• •

A rabbi was telling a group of young children in kindergarten class the story of Lot's wife, who turned into a pillar of salt when she disobeyed her husband and looked back at the destruction of Sodom. The children sat amazed. Then the rabbi asked the little ones, "Have you ever heard of anything so amazing when a person doesn't listen to a warning?"

One little one raised her hand and exclaimed, "I know a story that is even worse than that!"

The rabbi said, "Oh, please go ahead and tell us."

The little one continued, "My daddy was giving my mother

driving lessons. He kept warning her not to look back. But she didn't listen and turned into a telephone pole."

. . . .

A small boy was having an argument with his father about a raise in his weekly stipend. "Dad," he complained, "For a $600 tax deduction, I think I deserve more than a quarter."

. . . .

A sweet little old lady walked into a bank with a check that her son had sent her and asked to have the check cashed. The teller looked at the check and noticed it was not endorsed.

"I'm sorry madam, but this check is not endorsed. You have to sign it."

The old lady was confused as she had never had any business with a bank. "Why do I have to sign it? It came from my son in Chicago."

The teller understood and commented, "Well, you have to sign it so that your son will know you got the check!"

She then handed the check to the teller, who looked at the endorsement and smiled understandingly.

The endorsement read, 'Irving, I got the check. Love, Mama!'

A sweet old grandmother was walking along the beach with her 3-year-old grandson. Suddenly, the little one pulled away from his grandmother and raced into the surf. Just at that minute, a big wave came, and the little fellow disappeared under the water.

The old lady screamed and the life-guards ran into the water, fighting the tremendous waves and rocks and managed to find and rescue the little fellow.

The life-guard, all out of breath, brought the child to the grandmother's side and said, "Here's your grandson, Ma'am."

The old lady grabbed the child's hand, then looked at the life-guard and said, "He had a hat!"

. . . .

A teacher asked a group of her little ones the definition of the word 'housework.' One little one raised her hand and declared, "Housework is what a Mommy does that nobody notices until she doesn't do it!"

. . . .

A teenager turned to his father one day and asked, "Hey Pop, how much was the most money you earned in one year?"

The old man looked up from his newspaper and said, "Ask your mother, I forgot what I told her."

A 3-year-old was wandering through a downtown department store, crying. A security guard went over to the child and said, "Why are you crying?"

The little one sniffed and said, "I can't find my mommy!"

The security guard said, "I'll help you find her. What's your name? What does your mommy call you?"

The little one exclaimed, *"Mein Shayne Punim!"*

. . . .

A very distraught mother rushed her little 5-year old son, Izzy, to her doctor's office.

"Dr. Goldberg, tell me, can a child my Izzy's age take out an appendix?"

The doctor smiled very warmly and declared, "Why of course not, Mrs. Levine, why do you ask?"

"Never mind," she retorted. Then looking at the child, she exclaimed, *"Nu,* see, I told you — so put it back!"

. . . .

A young lady, who was in an obvious family way, stopped off in Boro Park to make a purchase. The salesgirl, in order to make light conversation, smiled and asked, "Are you expecting?"

The young lady smiled warmly and replied, "No, I'm not expecting — I'm certain!"

A young man, who had made it in business, wanted to make certain his father was taken care of as well as possible, so he stopped off in the finest men's shop in the city and bought his father a beautiful camel's hair coat. It was exquisite and cost over $500.

Realizing that his father, a very frugal man, would not accept such an extravagant gift, he had the storeowner remove the $500 price tag and put a tag on the coat that read $19.98. Then, he sent the coat to his father.

A few days later, he called his father and asked, "Pop, did you get the coat I sent you?"

The old man replied, "Yes, it was beautiful! See if you can pick up another, I sold this one to my neighbor for $25!"

. . . .

A young man who just graduated from medical school, went to Israel and called his mother.

"Ma, I just joined the Israeli Army as a doctor!"

The mother was all excited. "That's wonderful! Tell me, *tateleh*, did they at least give you a commission?"

The son thought for a moment, then said, "Na, I just get a salary like everyone else."

. . . .

A young man, who lived on Long Island, had his father live with him. The two went to shul every Shabbos. The old timer had the habit of dozing while the rabbi spoke, and the young man became embarrassed.

One day, he hit upon a plan. He had his young son sit next to the old timer and promised to give him a nickel after Shabbos if he prevented his grandfather from falling asleep.

All went well for a few weeks…then it started all over again. The old timer kept dozing whenever the rabbi spoke. After services, the young man approached his son and asked, "Look, I made a deal with you. I promised to give you a nickel every time you kept Zeidy awake, so what happened?"

The little boy looked up and explained, "Yeah, but Zeidy offered me a dime not to disturb him!"

. . . .

A young mother called to her 4-year-old son, "Shloimy, did you give the goldfish fresh water?"

The little one called back, "Didn't have to. They didn't drink what I gave them yesterday."

. . . .

A young mother, trying to teach her little one arithmetic, was sitting with the child at the kitchen table and asked, "Tell me *tateleh*, if Papa earned $1,000 a week and gave Mommy half, what would Mommy have?"

The little one thought for a moment then replied, "Heart failure!"

A young mother was admonishing her 5-year-old son for telling lies. "Irving, do you know what happens to little children who tell lies?"

The little one turned, and without batting an eyelash, snapped, "Yes, they run for public office."

. . . .

A young woman at the supermarket was pushing a full cart. A baby rode in the seat, and she held a husky, older-than-two-year-old youngster on her hip.

"My goodness!" exclaimed the checker, "Can't that big boy walk?"

"He certainly can!" the young mother replied, "Why do you think I am carrying him?"

. . . .

An 8-year-old was asked to write a composition on Father's Day. After giving it some thought, he wrote, "He can climb the highest mountain or swim the biggest ocean. He can fly the fastest plane and fight the strongest tiger. But most of the time, he just takes out the garbage."

. . . .

An insurance broker was giving his daughter driving lessons. As they were coming down a steep hill, she shouted, "The brakes aren't holding! What do I do?"

The broker shouted, "Brace yourself and aim for something cheap!"

. . . .

An Italian gentleman met a friend on the street and proudly announced that his sister had given birth to twins — a boy and a girl.

"That's lovely," said his friend. "What do they call the children?"

The Italian gentleman replied, "We call the girl Denise..."

"And the boy?" asked the friend.

"Oh," smiled the Italian, "Denephew!"

. . . .

An old rabbi was walking down the street and saw a little boy struggling on his tippy-toes to reach a doorbell. The rabbi walked up and rang the bell for the child.

"Thanks, Rabbi," the child commented, "Now we run!"

. . . .

An old timer got on a train and sat down next to another old timer. "Excuse me," the old man began with great hesitation. "Do you have any grandchildren?"

The second old timer smiled broadly and replied, "Yes. I have three wonderful grandchildren!"

The first old timer smiled uneasily, got up, and moved on to another seat, where another middle-aged man was sitting.

"Pardon me," the old timer said softly, "Do you have any grandchildren?" The man smiled and said, "Oh, yes! Indeed, I have four wonderful grandchildren."

The old man smiled once more, got up and sat down next to another younger looking man.

He turned to the man and asked once more, "Pardon me, do you have any grandchildren?"

The young man replied, "Why, not yet."

The old man smiled broadly and replied, "That's good! Now let me tell you about mine..."

· ·

And did you hear the story of the Martian who landed on Long Island one summery day and walked over to a man and said, "Take me to your leader."

And the man answered, "I can't — she's in South Fallsburg with the children!"

· ·

As little Irving was going to sleep, his mother peeked through the door to see if he was saying his prayers. Indeed, he was deep in thought. She heard him say, "And another thing, G-d, could you please put vitamins in ice cream, sodas, and cake instead of vegetables and meat?"

Catching her 3-year-old granddaughter in the act of eating her sister's grapes, the grandmother confronted her.

"Are you eating your little sister's grapes?"

"No," the 3-year-old innocently replied. "I'm helping her to share."

. . . .

Chana Finkleberg called her doctor and exclaimed, "Doctor, doctor, my little Irving just swallowed a pen. What should I do?"

The doctor replied, "I'll be right over."

"But what should I do in the meantime?" she asked frantically.

"Use a pencil!" the doctor replied.

. . . .

Chykeh was telling a woman she just met in the Catskills about her wonderful family. "We have three wonderful children, five grandchildren, and three great grandchildren... G-d bless them. And how many children do you have?" she asked her friend.

The other woman smiled uneasily and said, "Well, we never had any children."

Chykeh, sighed, "*Oy*...so what do you do for aggravation?"

Cohen was proudly expounding the virtues of his son. "My Irving is a lawyer of the first order; only the biggest come to him. And my Seymour, you should see from your children what I see from my Seymour. He's a doctor, bless him. When patients come to him and they can't afford an operation, he touches up the x-rays. And my Solly — he's a professor in an Engineering School. The biggest! They sent for him in Israel to build a canal next to the Suez. Very bright boy!"

"And you," his friend asked, "What do you do?"

"Me?" Cohen sighed, "I'm nothing but a lowly tailor. I have a small store, but I manage to support them all!"

• •

Cohen was talking to a friend. "Let me tell you something. I have a son, G-d bless him. He certainly is a help. You know, I run a small business, and business has been bad. *Nu*, so immediately after my son got out of college, he went to work with me in the business. And he wasn't there three months when he really put me on my feet!"

"The boy is such a business genius?" the friend asked.

"Not exactly," the first fellow explained, "You see, he borrowed my car the first week, wrapped it around a pole and I have been forced to walk ever since!"

• •

During a visit to a Jewish day school, a rabbi asked some of the toddlers, "Do you say your prayers every night before you go to sleep?"

"Oh, no," smiled the child, "My mommy does."

"What does she say?" asked the rabbi.

"Thank heavens he's in bed!" replied the child.

. . . .

Evelyn Mermelstein tells the story of being concerned over the fact that her 6-year-old hadn't spoken a word since he was born. One day, the youngster was having breakfast and turned to her, exclaiming, "Hey Mom, this toast is a little too dry!"

"Junior, you talked!" she exclaimed, "You talked! How come you never talked before?"

"Well," explained the little one, "Up to now, everything's been okay!"

. . . .

Goldberg met an old friend on the street. "Listen...last time I saw you, you told me your son was a doctor, so all of a sudden I find out he's an undertaker."

"I didn't lie to you," replied his friend, "All I said was he follows the medical profession!"

. . . .

I once asked an obstetrician how he sets his fees. "Well," he explained, "I have two fees. I send a bill for either $500 or $1,000."

"Well, how do you determine the fee?" I questioned. "Do you look up their financial rating or do you ask about their incomes?"

"Neither," he explained. "I base my fee on what the father says when I come out of the delivery room. If the father asks, "Is it a boy or a girl?" I bill him $1,000. If he asks, "Is my wife alright?" I bill him just $500!"

* *

In the mountains, two modern grandmothers were exclaiming the virtues of their children. "My daughter Sophie married some boy!" exclaimed Mrs. Finkelstein. "He's in the stock market and they have four cars!"

The other woman was impressed. "Do they have any children?" she asked.

"Of course," Mrs. Finkelstein explained. "G-d bless him — I have a grandchild 15 months old!"

"Does he walk?" asked the other woman.

"Why should he?" exclaimed Mrs. Finkelstein. "With four cars, he should walk?"

* *

It was a beautiful day in the park, and a young father was pushing his little one in a baby carriage while the little one was screaming his head off. As the father wheeled the carriage, he kept saying very softly, "Easy now, Shloimy. Just keep calm. Shloimy, please, steady. Shloimy, it's okay. Just relax, Shloimy..."

Just then, a woman passed by and said to the father, "You certainly know how to talk to and calm an upset child ever so quietly and gently." She then leaned over the carriage, smiled to the baby and asked, "What seems to be the trouble, Shloimy?"

The father interrupted her, "He's Yitzchok. I'm Shloimy!"

. . . .

Little Herby was an angel. His grandmother was babysitting him one night while his mother and father were attending a shul meeting. When the parents came home, they asked the little one, who was still up, "Did anybody call?"

The child thought for a minute, then said, "Oh, a man came to the door and asked if we could give him something for an old age home."

"*Nu*, so what did you do?" the mother beamed.

The little one shrugged. "So I gave him Grandma!"

. . . .

Little Irving phoned his father and tearfully exclaimed, "Daddy, Aunt Tova ran over my bicycle when she was backing the car out of the driveway this morning!"

The unsympathetic father replied, "How many times have I warned you not to leave your bicycle in the middle of the front lawn?"

Little Irving came running into the house with tears streaming down his face.

"What's the matter, *tateleh*?" his mother asked sympathetically.

"Papa was hammering a nail in the door and just hit his thumb with a hammer!" the little one sobbed.

"That's a reason to cry?" the mother consoled. "A big boy like you shouldn't cry at a trifle like that. Why didn't you just laugh?"

"I did!" sobbed little Irving.

. . . .

Little Irving's mother walked into the bedroom and saw the child with his finger in a bandage. "What happened, darling?" she asked.

"I hit my finger with a hammer," the child whimpered.

"How come I didn't hear you cry?" she asked.

"I thought you were out!" the child tearfully explained.

. . . .

Little Irving was out in the garden, trying to pull a weed out of the ground. His mother looked out the window and smiled, "You must be pretty strong trying to pull that weed out of the ground all by yourself!"

The little fellow paused for a moment and then looked up.

"Yup — I sure am — especially since the whole world is pulling on it from the other side!"

* * * * *

Mrs. Rosenfeld's son had struck it rich and was mixing with the *hoi polloi*. One day, he phoned his mother and said, "Ma, you know who I met yesterday?"

"*Nu*, so who did you meet?" the old lady asked.

"I met Picasso!" the son replied.

"Picasso? The fruit man?" the old lady asked.

"Ma, Picasso the painter!" the son snapped back.

"Oh, very nice," the old lady commented, "Find out how much he'll charge to do the kitchen and the bathroom!"

* * * * *

My son recently observed that men are smarter than women. When I asked him why, he commented, "Did you ever see a man who bought a shirt that buttoned down the back?"

* * * * *

A proud grandmother was wheeling a toddler in a stroller and holding the hand of another tot at her side. "How adorable," a neighbor exclaimed, "Your grandchildren? How old are they?"

The proud grandmother beamed, "G-d bless them, the lawyer is two and the doctor is going to be five."

. . . .

Sadie to Sarah: "Do your daughters live at home?"

Sarah to Sadie: "No, they're not married yet."

. . . .

Sadie was telling her mother how considerate her husband Irving was. "So tell me," her mother asked, "When the baby cries at night, who gets up?"

The girl thought for a minute and replied, "The whole building!"

. . . .

Sadie was waiting by a bus stop when an old friend stopped by. "Hello, Sadie," the friend began, "I haven't seen you in years. *Nu*, so how's your husband?"

Sadie shrugged, "How could he be?"

"And your children — I understand your oldest son graduated from medical school. *Nu*, so how is he doing?"

Sadie shrugged, "How could he be doing — he graduated from medical school."

"And your daughter? I understand she got married and made you a grandmother."

"*Nu*, so how should a grandmother be?"

Just then the bus arrived, and the friend turned to Sadie and said warmly, "*Oy*, it's such a pleasure to meet an old friend and have a heart-to-heart talk!"

· ·

Sadie went shopping with her little one, Stanley. When they came to the fruit store, the fruit man said, "Stanley, would you like a few grapes as a free treat?"

The youngster nodded yes.

"So take a handful," the fruit man suggested.

The youngster hesitated.

Finally, the fruit man put his hand in the pile of grapes and handed a huge bunch to the child.

When they left the store, the mother said, "Stanley, why didn't you take a handful of grapes when he asked you?"

"Because his hand was bigger than mine!" exclaimed the little one.

· ·

The doting grandmother was trying to get her little grandson to eat his spinach. "*Ess tateleh*," she said, "Make believe it's mud."

· ·

The head of a large firm went into his Accounts Receivable department and went over to the new employee.

"I want to tell you, Mrs. Rosenberg, your letters to those who owe us money are remarkable. Where did you get all those wonderful approaches? You have gotten money out of people who have owed us for years!"

The woman smiled. "Simple! I just compiled portions from the letters my son wrote to me from college!"

• •

The kindergarten teacher greeted her children the first day of school. "When I call your name, please give me your father's name. Isaac Rabinowitz..." she called.

The little one answered, "Papa."

"No, no," smiled the teacher. "What names does your mother call your father?"

The little one sighed, "Nothing. They don't fight!"

• •

The little one ran into the house and asked his mother, "Mommy, is a chicken big enough to eat when it's two weeks old?"

The mother laughed, "Of course not, it's too small."

The little one then asked, "So how does it manage to live?"

• •

The year is 2012 and the United States of America has recently elected Susan Goldfarb as the first woman, as well as the first Jewish president. She calls up her mother a few weeks after Election Day and says, "So, Mom, I assume you will be coming to my inauguration?"

"I don't think so, darling. It's a 10-hour drive, your father isn't as young as he used to be, and my arthritis is acting up."

"Don't worry, Mom. I'll send Air Force One to pick you up and take you home. And a limousine will wait at your door."

"I don't know...everybody will be so fancy-shmantzy. I have only *shmattes* in my closet!"

"Oh, Mom," replies Susan, "I'll make sure you have a wonderful gown by a famous designer."

"Sweetheart," Mom complains, "You know I can't eat those foods they eat at those fancy-shmantzy events."

The President-to-be responds, "Don't worry, Mom, the entire affair is going to be handled by the best kosher caterer in New York. Mom — I really want you to come!"

So Mom reluctantly agrees. On January 20, 2013, Susan Goldfarb is being sworn in as President of the United States of America. In the front row sits the new president's mother and father. Leaning over, Susan's mother whispers to a Senator sitting next to her.

"You see that woman over there with her hand on the Bible, who is just becoming the next President of the United States?" The Senator politely whispers back, "Yes ma'am, I certainly do."

Mom beams proudly and announces, "Well, her brother is a doctor!"

The young mother looked at her little one as he sat down to dinner. "Irving, tell me, your face is spotless and clean, but your hands are filthy. How did you get your hands so dirty?"

The little one replied, "From washing my face!"

. . . .

There was a banging on the door of Hockmeyer's apartment. Mrs. Hockmeyer opened the door and saw her little Irving's friends. "Mrs. Hockmeyer," the children gasped frantically, "We were playing a game who could lean out the hall window the furthest."

"So?" interrupted Mrs. Hockmeyer, "Why all the excitement?"

"Irving won!" stammered the little ones.

. . . .

Two little ones were talking and one asked, "How old is your grandfather?"

The second one replied, "I really don't know, but we've had him for a very long time!"

. . . .

Uncle Shmuel was trying to teach one of his little nephews a moral. He put two cookies on a plate in front of the child. One was a little larger than the other. Then he said to one of the little ones, "Here are two cookies. One is for you and one for me. You take one first."

The little one took the larger cookie. Uncle Shmuel asked, "Was that proper, taking the larger one and leaving the smaller one for me?"

The little one sighed and asked, "And what cookie would you have taken if you picked first?"

The uncle smiled, "Why? I certainly would have taken the smaller one and left the larger one for you!"

The little one sighed once more, "*Nu*, so isn't that the one I took?"

Education

· ·

A chemistry teacher was showing his class different types of powerful acids. He picked up a glass and said, "I am going to drop a gold ring into this solution; will it dissolve or not?"

The student shot back, "It will not!"

The teacher said, "How do you know?"

The student replied, "Because you wouldn't drop the ring in it if it did!"

· ·

A first grade teacher was shocked when one of her little ones told her that the boys were throwing cats into the

river. A few minutes later, one of the little ones wandered into class.

"Why are you so late?" the teacher demanded.

The little one replied, "I cannot tell a lie. Um, I was throwing cats into the river."

"That's terrible," the teacher said. "Stay after class!"

In a few minutes, another little boy came into the room. "Why are you late?" the teacher asked.

"I was throwing cats into the river."

The teacher was exploding. "You, too, stay after class!"

Then another little fellow came into the classroom.

"And I suppose you were throwing cats in the river also?" the teacher shouted.

"No," said the little one, "I'm Katz!"

. . . .

A friend of mine reminded me of the story of the young lady who made an application to teach in a new school. The principal of that school called the principal of the school she said she previously taught in.

"Excuse me — could you tell me how long she taught in your school?"

The principal in the other school replied, "One day."

The first principal gasped, "But on her application, she says she was in your school for 5 years."

The second principal sighed, "That's true. But to your question how long she taught — she taught one day!"

. . . .

A Jewish traveling salesman is passing through the mountains of Kentucky and he stops off at a hillbilly's home. He starts to talk to an old timer named Zeke.

"Is that your son out there milking the cow?" the salesman asks.

The hillbilly nods, "Yup. Lem's my son."

The salesman says, "He appears to be a smart boy and should get an education. My father runs a Judaica shop in Brooklyn. He could use a strong, young boy. Maybe your son could work in my father's shop during the day and we will pay for his education, give him room and board, and he will be able to go to school at night."

The old hillbilly is convinced. So, the boy leaves for Brooklyn, and for the next four years works in the Judaica shop and goes to college.

Finally, he returns home after he graduates from college. He meets his father at the train. The old hillbilly smiles and says, "Well son, tell me the truth, did you really change?"

The young man puts his arm around his father and says, "Listen, Abba, vonce ah hillbilly, alvays ah hillbilly!"

A kindergarten class was getting ready to go home. One little one began to cry as she struggled to put on a pair of boots. The teacher got down on her hands and knees and began to struggle with the boots. After a few minutes, she breathed a sigh of relief as the boots were finally put on the child's feet.

"Well, that wasn't too bad!" the teacher exclaimed, blotting her brow. "Now, why were you still crying?"

The little one looked up and continued crying, "...because they're not my boots!"

. . . .

A rather innovative teacher asked her third grade class to write a sentence beginning with the word "Than." All but one of the kids were stuck. The one little resourceful youngster wrote, "Than is a word with four letters."

. . . .

A school principal phoned the parents of a youngster who did not feel well in class. The phone rang and was answered by an obviously little boy.

The principal said, "Is your mother or father home?"

The little one replied, "No."

"Well, is there anyone else there I can speak with?" the principal asked.

The little boy on the phone replied, "Yeh, my sister."

So the principal says, "Can I speak to her?"

And the little boy said, "Yeh."

So the principal waits and waits and finally, after a long period of silence, the little boy gets back on the phone and says, "I can't lift her out of the crib!"

. . . .

A school teacher asked her little ones, "Now tell me, what one thing can you do better than anyone else?"

A little boy raised his hand and replied, "Read my own handwriting!"

. . . .

A school teacher, for homework, assigned his students a handful of words to be looked up in the dictionary.

"Pa," the youngster began, "What's the difference between 'anger' and 'exasperation?'"

The father smiled and explained, "Well, it is really a matter of semantics. But, let me show you."

He went to the telephone and dialed a set of numbers arbitrarily. The phone buzzed and, even though the hour was late, someone answered.

The father asked, "Hello, is Chaim there?"

The voice on the phone replied, "I'm sorry, there's no Chaim here — you have the wrong number. You'd better check with the operator!"

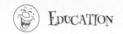

The father apologized and hung up the phone.

"See," exclaimed the father, "That man really wasn't angry, but you could say he was sort of exasperated. Now we'll call him again and see what happens."

He dialed the same number again. The phone was picked up as the father said, "Hello, is Chaim there?"

"Now, listen Mister," the voice shouted heatedly, "You still have the wrong number! I told you before, there is no Chaim here! You have a lot of nerve calling at this hour of the night! Call information for the number and, for crying out loud, stop bothering me!"

The father turned to the son and said, "Now I'll show you the difference between exasperation and true anger."

And, so, for the third time, he dialed the number. In a second, the phone buzzed, and an angry voice came on, "HELLO!" it shouted.

The father calmly exclaimed, "Hello, this is Chaim, any messages for me?"

. . . .

A school teacher, in an effort to teach her children to think, announced one day, "From now on, every Friday, just before we go home, I will ask one question. Whoever knows the correct answer will be excused from school on Monday!"

The children cheered and couldn't wait until Friday came. Then, on Friday, two minutes before school ended, the teacher stood up and announced, "Now for the question. Whoever answers this correctly can take Monday off! All right," she began, as the children listened intently. "Who can tell me, to within one million, how many grains of sand there are on Beach 25th Street in Coney Island?"

The little ones began to guess, "A trillion," shouted one. "A billion billion," shouted another.

"I'm sorry, no one got the right answer, so I'll see you all on Monday," she chuckled.

The following Friday, she stood at the desk and asked, "Who can tell me how many stars there are in the heavens?" Again the little ones guessed and guessed, but none could come up with the answer.

The following week, the children waited with anticipation. Then, just a second before the teacher was to rise to give her weekly question, one of the little ones threw a paper airplane and it landed on the teacher's desk. Indignantly, she rose and asked, "Who threw that?"

Little Irving stood up and said, "I did! — See you on Tuesday!"

. . . .

A school teacher was puzzled when a pupil brought a note from home asking that he be excused from school due to a religious holiday. She phoned the mother and asked, "What religious holiday?"

"Oh," the mother explained, "That's the holiday we're taking to see the circus — we go there every year religiously."

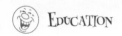

A student approached his teacher and asked, "Why did you give me a zero on our last test? Almost all my answers were correct."

The teacher explained, "That's true, but didn't you copy your answers from Yankel, who was sitting next to you?"

"That's true," the student said apologetically. "But how did you know?"

The teacher replied, "Your answers and Yankel's were exactly the same except for one. For that one, Yankel wrote, 'I don't know,' and you wrote, 'I don't know, either!'"

. . . .

A teacher asked her little ones, "Who can name five things that contain milk?"

One youngster raised her hand and said, "Ice cream, butter, cheese, and two cows!"

. . . .

A teacher, explaining the use of the singular and the plural in grammar, asked one youngster, "Seymour, can you tell me, is the word 'pants' singular or plural?"

The youngster thought for a moment, then exclaimed, "Both! — Singular at the top and plural at the bottom!"

A teacher was questioning Abie, a star pupil in her class. "Abie, how many make a dozen?"

"Twelve," replied Abie.

"And how many make a million?" continued the teacher.

"Very few," said Abie.

• •

A university professor was teaching foreign students and wanted to encourage them to present individual views on any subject, so he suggested they write a paper about elephants.

"I want your thinking on the subject according to your own national perspective," the instructor concluded.

A few days later, the German student came with a paper entitled, "The Elephant in Warfare."

A French student wrote, "The Culinary Life of the Elephant."

A student from England submitted a paper entitled, "Elephant Hunting."

A student from UCLA wrote, "The Elephant and the Unjust Israeli Occupation."

• •

A youngster was asked by his teacher if he said his prayers before each meal. The little one looked up proudly and exclaimed, "I don't have to. My mother is a good cook!"

An English teacher was asking her group of little ones to explain opposites.

"Irving, can you tell me the opposite of joy?"

The little one said, "Misery."

"Now what is the opposite of sorrow?" the teacher asked.

Another little one exclaimed, "Happiness!"

"Now comes the hard one," the teacher exclaimed. "What is the opposite of woe?"

One little one raised his hand, then hesitated for a moment. The teacher asked once more, "Come now, what is the opposite of woe?"

Without batting an eye, the little one replied, "Giddyup!"

. . . .

An experienced teacher announced to his students, "And, for today's lecture, we will discuss liars. Now, how many of you have read the 25th chapter in our text?" All but two hands were raised.

The old timer smiled warmly and added, "That's excellent — I can now see that my topic is well taken. There is no 25th chapter in our text!"

. . . .

And the cutest little quip of all came from my own little son, who started in nursery school. After the first day, I asked him, "*Nu*, so what did you learn in school today?"

And the little one's eyes opened like two saucers, as he exclaimed, "Apparently not enough...I gotta go again tomorrow!"

. . . .

At a summer camp, a lifeguard wanted to impress upon one of his little campers the importance of water safety. He asked one of his charges, "Suppose your school took a boat ride up the Hudson River. All the teachers and students were on that boat. Now tell me, what would you do if one of the teachers accidentally fell overboard?"

The child thought for a moment, then asked, "Which one?"

. . . .

Before sending her son off for his first day at school, Rachel Cohen hugged him and said, "Good luck, my *bubbeleh*. Be good, *bubbeleh*, and work hard. And remember, *bubbeleh*, at lunchtime eat all of your food and play nicely with the other children. Oh, *bubbeleh*, I'm so proud!"

That afternoon, when little Cohen returned home, his mother cried, "*Bubbeleh*, my *bubbeleh*, give your mother a hug! So, tell me, what did you learn at school today?"

"Well," said the boy, "To start with, I learned that my name is Sammy!"

Did you ever hear the story of how 'NYU' got its name? Nachum Ungeshstopped had come to our shores many years ago. Knowing no one here, and without resources, he started out as a peddler. Sure enough, good fortune smiled upon him. He earned enough money to open a small novelty store. And then through ambition and hard work, he opened another store and then another, until he had a chain of over 1,000 stores all over the country.

Little by little, he brought over his relatives from Europe, gave them jobs, and, eventually, formed partnerships with each. Finally, one day, he decided to fulfill his lifelong ambition of endowing a University in this great nation.

One afternoon, at a Board of Director's meeting with all his relatives seated around the huge Board of Director's table, he announced, "My partners, I've decided to endow a new University in our great city."

All the relatives applauded.

"And now for the name," Nachum announced, "I think, since there are too many of you to be included in the name, I'll call it the Nachum Yitzchok Ungeshtopped University."

Just then, his cousin, annoyed at being left out, exclaimed, "Un' why you?"

Nachum thought for a second, then exclaimed, "You know. I like that better!"

And from that day on, it's been known on the Lower East Side as 'un why you!'

Four high school students, who had to take a final exam in math, decided to skip their morning class. They figured they would ask some of the other kids what were the questions on the test.

When they arrived, they pleaded with their teacher that they were going to be in school at the right time, but they were late because they had a flat tire on the way.

Much to their relief, the teacher smiled and said, "Well, since you missed the test this morning, please take a piece of paper and sit three seats apart from each other."

When everything was set, the teacher said, "For your test, there will only be one question. If you get it right, you will pass. If you don't, you will fail. Are you ready?"

They all smiled. "Yes, teacher."

"Now here's the question: Which tire was flat?"

. . . .

Grandpa asks his little grandson, "Well, how do you like school?"

The little one sighed, "Mostly when it's closed."

. . . .

In old Russia, the military swooped down on a yeshiva and inducted the entire student body into the army. When the Russians gave them training, they were flabbergasted at the amazing target marksmanship of the youths.

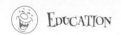

The military placed the entire student body of the yeshiva on the front lines.

When they arrived at the front, the line officer shouted one day, "Ready...aim...fire!!!"

But nothing happened.

"Fire!!!" shouted the officer.

Still nothing happened.

Burning with rage, he turned to the students and shouted, "Why don't you shoot?"

One of the youths innocently replied, "Can't you see...there are people in the way — someone might get hurt!"

. . . .

In one of the New York universities, a young yeshiva boy registered and began taking courses. In every class he would address the instructor as "Honored Professor."

One day, one of the other students called him aside and said, "Look, at a university, an instructor is addressed simply as 'Mr.' or 'Mrs.' or 'Dr.' — only the head of a department or an extremely learned and educated person is addressed as 'Professor.'"

The young man smiled meekly and said softly, "If it's all the same to you, you get your A's your way, and I'll get mine my way!"

Little Irving came running home from school one day, waving a piece of paper with some scribbles on it.

"Mommy, Mommy, look! Today we learned how to write."

The mother looked at the scribble on the page and beamed. "Oh, *vee shain!* And what does it say, *tateleh?*"

The little one sighed, "I don't know, we don't learn to read until tomorrow."

. . . .

Little Irving was busily drawing a picture in the nursery school when his teacher looked over his shoulder and asked, "And what are you drawing?"

The little fellow continued coloring and scribbling away, but he managed to say, "I'm drawing a picture of G-d."

The teacher, surprised, warmly explained, "But no one knows what G-d looks like."

The little one looked up innocently, thought a moment, and then added, "They will after I finish this picture!"

. . . .

Little Shmully came home from school earlier than usual. His mother asked, "Shmully darling, how come you came home from school so early?"

Shmully replied, "I was the only one who could answer a certain question."

The mother was so thrilled. "And what was that question?" "The principal wanted to know who threw the eraser at him…"

Mrs. Goldman, a sixth-grade teacher, posed the following problem to one of her arithmetic classes:

"A wealthy man dies and leaves $10 million. One-third is to go to his wife, one-fifth is to go to his son, one-sixth is to go to his butler, one-eighth to his secretary, and the rest to charity. Now, what does each get?"

The teacher called on little Moishy for his answer. With complete sincerity in his voice, Moishy answered, "A good lawyer!"

So, the school teacher was doing an arithmetic exercise. She turned to little Montgomery Finkelstein and asked, "Tell me, if your father's business partner borrowed $100 and promised to pay back the money on a basis of $10 a week, how much would he owe at the end of 8 weeks?"

The youngster replied, "$200!"

"I'm afraid you don't know your lesson very well," snapped the teacher.

"And you don't know my father's business partner very well!" explained the youngster.

The teacher was teaching proverbs and exclaimed to her students, "Cleanliness is next to what?"

"Impossible!" exclaimed a little one with feeling.

. . . .

The kindergarten teacher asked one of her little ones, "Do you say your prayers every night when you go to bed?"

The little one looked up and commented, "I don't have to. My Mommy says them for me."

"Your mother says them for you?" questioned the teacher. "What does she say when you go to sleep?"

The little one sighed, "She says, 'Thank heavens he's in bed!'"

. . . .

The mother of a young man comes to his bedside and says, "You have to get up and go to school, darling."

The young man blinks and says, "I don't want to go to school!"

"Why?" the mother asks.

"Nobody likes me at school," the young man moans. "The teachers don't like me, and even the kids don't like me. The superintendent wants to transfer me, and even the bus drivers hate me. And, believe it or not, even the custodian has it in for me. So, I don't wanna go anymore."

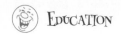

The mother says, "But you have to go to school, darling. You're the principal!"

. . . .

The professor was trying to teach his students how to remember names. "All you have to do is associate things that would normally go with the name. For example, if you met a Mr. Baker, you would associate his name with baking. If you met Mr. Gold, associate his name with, say, jewelry or a gold ring."

"But what happens if I meet somebody by the name of Machashevitzberg?" asked the student.

"Don't get too friendly!" exclaimed the professor.

. . . .

The teacher was reading little Golda's homework. She looked up in despair and sighed, "This has so many errors, I can't understand how one kid could have made all those mistakes."

The little one looked up and said, "One person didn't. My brother helped me!"

. . . .

The teacher was trying to explain logical thinking to his students. So, he posed a question. If the distance between New York and Philadelphia is about 100 miles, how far is it from Philadelphia to New York?"

One student raised his hand and exclaimed, "What

difference does it make whether it is New York to Philadelphia, or Philadelphia to New York? The distance backward or forward would be the same."

The teacher smiled and explained, "That is not always true. You see, it is only one month between Purim and Passover, but from Passover to Purim it is eleven months!"

• •

The two cloak manufacturers met for lunch in New York City's Garment Center.

"Sam." the first began, "I understand your son has been accepted at a very fancy university."

"Of course," explained Sam, "The boy is brilliant."

"Tell me," the first fellow questioned. "*Nu*, so what will he be when he graduates?"

Sam smiled proudly, "If the draft continues, probably about thirty-nine!"

• •

Two kids were talking, and one said to the other, "I flunked the test!"

"How far were you from the right answers?" asked the friend.

"About two seats away," the kid sighed.

The Pulpit

. . . .

A beggar stopped a well-dressed man on the street and asked for some money to get something to eat. The man said, "Tell you what, I'll buy you a drink."

The beggar said, "I don't drink."

The man said, "Well, then...here's a good cigar."

The beggar nodded a thank you and added, "I don't smoke."

The man said, "Look, I'll give you a tip on a sure winner at the race-track for this afternoon."

The beggar said, "I don't gamble."

The well-dressed man said, "In that case, come with me. I want to take you with me to show my rabbi what happens to a man who doesn't drink, smoke, or gamble!"

A famous cantor was invited to a very important synagogue to lead the High Holiday services. As he sang, tears began to fill his eyes. You could see he was singing with deep emotion.

After the services, the president of the shul walked over to the cantor and said candidly, "Tell me, Cantor, your singing was magnificent. I thought I even detected tears as you sang. Could you tell me what was running through your mind as you sang?"

The cantor breathed deeply and sighed, "I was counting the house!"

. . . .

A few old timers on the Board of Directors of a little *shteeble* were holding a meeting, when one of the members got up and announced, "Gentlemen, what our shul needs is a new chandelier."

A great debate soon followed. Finally, old Goldberg got up and shouted, "Enough of this! First of all, nobody here could even spell that word! Second, we got nobody here who could even play it! And third of all, what we need is not a chandelier, but a fixture for more light!"

. . . .

A friend of mine was given an award for outstanding service to his synagogue. In true modest fashion, he exclaimed, "I want to thank you all for this wonderful award and truthfully, I really don't deserve it."

He thought for a moment, then added, "Then again, I have bursitis in the shoulder and I don't deserve that, either."

· ·

Gabbai approaches a guest in shul and says, "I'd like to give you an *aliya* — what is your name?"

The man responds, "Sara bas Moshe."

The Gabbai says, "No, I need your name."

The man says, "It is Sara bas Moshe."

The Gabbai asks, "How can that be your name?"

The man answers, "I've been having serious financial problems and my lawyer said to put everything in my wife's name!"

· ·

local shul invited a very forceful speaker to address their congregation. The speaker was very emotional. He told of the great tragedies the Jews have suffered over the years and how infants were torn from their mothers' arms in the Holocaust. As he spoke, there wasn't a dry eye in the house.

When he had finished, he noticed one old timer, sitting in the back, who was not moved by his presentation. The speaker walked over to the man and asked, "Sir, you were the only one in this shul who was not moved by my speech. There were tears coming from every eye. How come you showed no emotion?"

The old timer simply shrugged, "I'm not a member here!"

A police officer was schmoozing with a rabbi when he asked him, "What is the quickest way to disperse a crowd?"

The rabbi smiled, "Announce an appeal!"

. . . .

A question was asked of a priest, a minister, and a rabbi. "When the time comes, and you are in your casket, and friends, family, and congregants are mourning over you, what you would like to hear them say?"

The Episcopal priest answered, "I would like to hear them say that I was a wonderful husband, a fine spiritual leader, and a great family man."

The Catholic priest said, "I would like to hear that I was a wonderful teacher and a servant of G-d, who made a huge difference in people's lives."

The rabbi answered, "I would like to hear them say, 'Look! He's moving!'"

. . . .

A rabbi and a cab driver meet at the gates of Heaven. The gatekeeper motions to the cab driver, "You can go right in." The rabbi protests, "Wait a minute! You're letting a cab driver in before me, a man of G-d?"

The gatekeeper says, "Rabbi, let me explain. Every Shabbos, when you give your sermon, two-thirds of your congregation doze off. Now, with this cab driver, not only did he never have anyone fall asleep in the back of his cab, but he actually had

many people who never prayed before praying with all their might while he drove!"

* *

A rabbi happened to see one of his congregants coming out of a local bar. The rabbi went over to the man and said, "Sam, let me ask you. Who has the most expensive house in this community?"

Sam replied, "The barkeeper — everybody knows that."

"And whose wife has the most expensive mink coat in our town?" the rabbi continued.

"The barkeeper's wife," he replied.

"And who has the largest bank account in this town?"

"You and I know — the barkeeper!"

The rabbi continued, "It's all the money from people like you in this town. Everybody brings their money to the barkeeper."

Sam hung his head in shame and walked away.

A few weeks later, Sam met the old rabbi once more, who said, "I guess my mini-sermon had its effect?"

"It sure did!" exclaimed Sam, "I just bought the place!"

* *

A rabbi I know, who is in constant demand as a speaker for various organizations, was asked by a friend, "You are rarely seen at your synagogue since you are all over the country speaking. How is it your congregation doesn't fire you?"

The rabbi smiled, "They have to find me first! "

. . . .

A rabbi was traveling cross country on a plane and began talking to the man sitting next to him. "I'm a rabbi..."

The man turned away for a moment and then smiled with sarcasm, "I really don't know too much about religion, but isn't religion summed up in that famous phrase, 'Love thy neighbor as thyself?'"

The rabbi, a little upset by the degree of generalization, asked, "And what do you do?"

The man said, "I'm an astrophysicist."

The rabbi thought for a moment and said, "I really don't know much about astrophysics, but can't the entire discipline be summarized in that famous phrase 'Twinkle Twinkle, little star?'"

. . . .

A rabbi was walking on the street and saw a little child playing with a ball. The old timer stopped and watched the child for a few minutes. "What are you doing?" the rabbi asked the little one, trying to make conversation.

"I'm playing ball with G-d!" the little fellow answered.

The rabbi began to laugh and asked, "Now, how in the world do you do that?"

The little one smiled and replied innocently, "Why, I throw the ball up to him, and he throws it down to me!"

* *

A rather wealthy man, who had a reputation of being a cheapskate, was quite ill and went to a doctor. The doctor gave him a medicine and said, "This is all I can do for you. If you begin to sweat, you will recover. But if not, it is then in G-d's hands."

A short time later, the rabbi came to the wealthy man's bedside. "I've come to pray for you," the rabbi said. "By the way," the rabbi continued, "The roof of our shul needs repairing..."

The wealthy man sighed, "Write down on a piece of paper that I am giving you $10,000 for the roof's repair."

The rabbi continued, "And there are about a hundred families in our community who barely have bread on their tables."

The wealthy man groaned, "...write down another $10,000 for the poor."

The rabbi went on, "...and there are ten widows with orphans who have no place to live..."

The wealthy man sighed once more, "...write down another $10,000 for the widows and orphans." Then he suddenly shouted, "Wait a minute! Wait a minute! Tear up the paper... I'm already sweating! I'm already sweating!"

A rather well-dressed man called on a rabbi and told him a distressing story of poverty and misery that was quite prevalent in the neighborhood.

"This poor widow," he said with tears streaming from his eyes, "with four tiny, starving children to feed, is sick in bed with no money for the doctor, no money for food and besides she owes $500 in rent for three months and is about to be evicted! I'm trying to raise the rent money for her. I wonder if you can help?"

"I certainly can," exclaimed the rabbi. "My friend, if you can give your time to this cause, so can I," and he handed him $500.

As the well-dressed man prepared to leave, the rabbi asked, "By the way, are you related to her?"

The man smiled sheepishly and replied, "No, I'm the landlord!"

· ·

A traveling salesman, driving through Louisiana, passed a little house in the middle of the woods. As he got closer, he saw a man dressed in typical rabbinical garb, standing on a porch and praying.

He approached the old timer and said, "This is amazing! Here in the middle of Louisiana — davening in the open!!"

The man smiled and said, "Let me explain. I am Rabbi Goldberg, and this place happens to be a Glatt Kosher restaurant. In Louisiana, putting up a sign that says it's a kosher restaurant might not go so well with the some in the community. So, the owners pay me to stay out here all day on the porch while I learn and daven. When tourists like yourself pass and see me, those who understand, stop for lunch or dinner."

The salesman was amazed. He went in and had a delicious meal and was back on the road once more. A few months later, he was driving through the wilds of Texas, and, sure enough, he saw the same rabbi sitting on another porch and davening once more.

He approached the rabbi and said, "What are you doing here?"

The rabbi shrugged his shoulders and said, "My boss did so well with the other restaurant that he decided to open one here, also. So now he pays me to do the same thing here. You see, this is also not the best place to advertise a Glatt Kosher restaurant."

The man agreed and went in for a meal. As he left, he said goodbye to the rabbi.

About a year later, the salesman was in Israel. As he was driving down a side street, he passed a beautiful hotel and saw the same Rabbi Goldberg sitting on the porch and davening. He scratched his head and approached Rabbi Goldberg, who stood up and greeted him.

"Now wait a minute," the salesman exclaimed, "I could understand in Louisiana where they couldn't put up a sign, they hired you. I could understand in Texas where they couldn't put up a sign also, so they hired you. But here, in Israel?"

The rabbi smiled and explained, "Here, I'm the golf pro!"

A visiting rabbi was giving a long-winded sermon. Suddenly, a loud snore was heard from the back of the shul. The rabbi turned indignantly to a member seated next to the snorer and said, "Will you please wake him up?"

The member shrugged, "Listen, you put him to sleep, you wake him up!"

- -

A wealthy man was sitting next to a very poor man in the synagogue. The poor man finished his prayers quickly, while the wealthy man still had a number of pages to go. When he finished, he turned to the poor man and asked, "Tell me, we both pray to G-d. But you go through those prayers so fast it is impossible for G-d to hear and understand your prayers."

The poor man sighed sadly and exclaimed, "You see, you don't understand. You are a wealthy man with a fine house, chauffeur, a fabulous business with many, many interests. I am a poor man with ten children in a 3-room apartment.

"When you pray to G-d, you have to ask him to preserve all the many things you have. That's why it takes you so long. But me, I only have to say two things, "wife — children" and I'm through!"

- -

A young boy had a habit of stealing lumber every time he passed a construction site. When he was finally arrested by the police, the family was advised to take him to a rabbi

who might explain the terrible thing he was doing in stealing all that lumber.

The rabbi who was chosen began to speak with the youth. He explained how wrong it was to steal the lumber from people who were trying to earn a living. After a while, it appeared as if the rabbi was making headway and the youth was beginning to understand.

Finally, the rabbi said, "My son, only through prayer and repentance can you come back to society."

The boy asked, "Rabbi, please tell me — how do I start?"

The rabbi exclaimed, "Well, do you know how to make a *bracha*?"

The boy thought for a moment and replied, "Well, if you got the plans, I got the lumber!"

. . . .

A young rabbi had invited the members of a nearby congregation, who were looking to hire a new rabbi, to visit his present shul to hear his sermon.

The young rabbi began his sermon and, as he spoke, he noticed the head of the auditioning committee beginning to doze off. After the service, the young rabbi approached the old timer who had come to hear him speak. "How in the world could you pass an opinion on my sermon when you were sound asleep for half the sermon?"

The old timer smiled meekly and replied, "When I fell asleep, I was expressing my opinion."

A young cantor was invited by a mental hospital to conduct services for the patients during the High Holidays. The Chief Psychiatrist of the hospital told the cantor to be prepared for anything and warned him to ignore any comments the patients might make during the services.

The cantor assured the Chief Psychiatrist that he would be able to handle the problem as it arose. He began the service and the patients listened. After a few minutes, one of the patients called out, "Gee whiz, that is the worst singing I have ever heard on Rosh Hashana!"

The cantor ignored the comment and continued. When he finished, the Chief Psychiatrist ran up to him and shook his hand. "You were wonderful! You have no idea how much you helped that man who called out."

"What are you talking about?" the cantor questioned. "He said my singing was the worst he had ever heard."

"That's just the point," exclaimed the psychiatrist, "That is the first rational statement that man has said in the past five years!"

. . . .

A young boy was watching his father, a rabbi, prepare his sermon. "How do you know what to write?" the little one asked.

The rabbi explained, "Well, I think a lot, and G-d tells me what to write."

The little one scratched his head for a moment, then asked, "Then why do you keep crossing things out?"

An Internal Revenue Service inspector walked into a synagogue and asked to see the rabbi. He is shown into the rabbi's study and offered a seat.

"Rabbi," said the inspector. "A member of your synagogue, a Mr. Klutz, states on his tax return that he has donated $100,000 to your synagogue. Is that correct?"

The rabbi answered, "Yes, he will!"

· ·

An old lady attending a Rosh Hashana service, paused in the middle of her prayers to offer a New Year greeting to G-d.

O, L-rd, what can I wish you?" she sighed. "I cannot wish you prosperity — for the whole world is Yours. I cannot wish You long life — for You will live forever. *Nu*, so all I can wish you is that you should have *Nachas* from your children."

· ·

An old time New York rabbi fulfilled his life's dream and went to Israel. The man was a wonderful person and could only find good in whatever he saw.

The greatest thrill of all was to be in Israel for the High Holidays. Sure enough, the old timer was walking toward the synagogue during Yom Kippur and saw a young man eating a sandwich.

The old timer walked over and said softly, "I suppose you didn't realize today is Yom Kippur, a day of fasting?"

The young man looked back and said, "No, I knew today was Yom Kippur."

"Then of course you know, for a Jew to eat on this day is a sin," the rabbi explained.

"Yes, I do," the young man returned.

"Then you must be a sick man and your doctor ordered you to eat every day and not to fast," the rabbi declared, searching for an answer.

"I'm in perfect health," exclaimed the young man.

The old timer smiled warmly and looked toward the heavens. "L-rd of the universe, what a remarkable land this is! Here in Israel, a Jew would rather admit that he is a sinner than tell a lie!"

"But I'm not Jewish," exclaimed the young man.

"*Noch Besser!*" exclaimed the old timer.

. . . .

As the services for a young boy's Bar Mitzvah came to a close, the rabbi handed the youth a beautiful siddur. The head of the Men's Club then stood up and gave the boy a beautiful Chumash. Finally, the head of the Sisterhood stood up and handed the boy an umbrella.

The rabbi looked at her and asked, "Why did you give him an umbrella?" She smiled and said, "I wanted to give him something he would at least open once in a while!"

Cohen was one of the best liked old timers on the shul's Board of Directors. He was controversial at times, but still respected. When he took ill and went to the hospital, the other members of the Board sent him a get-well note.

It read, "Dear Max. You will be very happy to know that the shul's Board of Directors wishes you a speedy recovery by a vote of 11 to 10, with two abstaining."

. . . .

Cohen was the head of the shul's fundraising committee and decided to visit the wealthiest man in town to see if he could get a donation for the shul. As he sat with the wealthy man, Cohen explained, "Mr. Goldberg, I've checked your Dunn and Bradstreet and see that you are doing very well. I have studied your firm's financial statement and see that you have made a sizable profit last year. Can you give us a donation for our shul?"

Goldberg leaned back in his chair and looked quite serious. "My good man, since you went through so much trouble to find out how much I'm worth, I'd like to fill you in on a few facts you may not know. I have a 90-year-old mother who has been in the hospital for ten years with round-the-clock nurses. I have a widowed daughter with six children and no means of support. My two brothers went into bankruptcy and owe the government thousands of dollars. Now, tell me, don't you believe that charity begins at home?"

Ashamed at having misjudged the wealthy man, Cohen explained apologetically, "I'm sorry. I had no idea you were saddled with so many family debts."

"I'm not," replied Goldberg, "But you must think I'm crazy to think I would give money to strangers when I won't even help my own relatives!"

• •

In every community there is a *kibbitzer* — one who likes to play his own little practical jokes. And so it was with Finkleberg, who went over to the President of his synagogue and exclaimed, "I guess you heard the committee held a meeting and decided to vote you out and appoint a new president in your place."

The President was filled with rage, "Who spoke against me?" he shouted.

"Well, there was Feldman, the contractor," the *kibbitzer* continued.

"Feldman?" screeched the President — "That nogoodnik. Why, that scoundrel has stolen millions from widows and orphans. He spoke against me? Who else?"

"Then there was also Shapiro — the banker," the kibbitzer replied.

"Shapiro? — That *goniff!* — He cheats everyone who goes to his bank! Who else spoke against me?" the President shouted with mounting anger.

"Then there was the principal of our Day School — you know, Rosenberg."

"Rosenberg — that ignoramous! He had the nerve to speak against me?" shouted the President, his face red as a beet.

At this point, the *kibbitzer* realized maybe he had gone too far and explained, "I was only kidding. In fact, when the committee met, every one of them spoke highly of you and said you were one of the finest men that has ever graced our shul's board."

The President settled back in his chair and sighed, "Now, why did you go and make me say those mean things about the finest group of men I have ever known?"

. . . .

In every congregation there are the question askers. There is always a small group who will dun a rabbi to death with questions.

One day, a congregant walked over to the rabbi and asked, "Rabbi, tell me why is it that on Passover we ask four questions but on Yom Kippur and Rosh Hashana we ask no questions?"

The old sage thought for a moment, then replied, "You see, to see a Jew cry and moan is not unusual and that raises no questions. But to see a Jew happy? That demands an explanation!"

. . . .

In one of the small Russian villages, there lived a brilliant rabbi. Every so often, the rabbi would visit the various communities delivering sermons and explain difficult portions of the law to scholars who sought knowledge. In every hamlet, great welcomes awaited the coming of this sage.

As they drove from village to village, the rabbi's driver

turned to the rabbi and said, "Rabbi, I admire you, and to tell the truth, I am jealous of the wonderful receptions they give you in each village. Oh, how I wish I could be honored in such a manner. I have an idea. Could you loan me your cloak and hat so that those in the next village will think I am you, the learned rabbi — just for this time?"

The rabbi was a merry old soul and was ready to go along with the plan but also realized the dangers.

"What if they ask you a question that you cannot answer? You will only make a fool of yourself," the rabbi said sagely.

"Don't worry!" said the driver, "I am certain I can take care of such problems."

So, the old rabbi exchanged clothes with the driver, and when they arrived in the next village, there was a great throng waiting to greet them. They ushered the 'rabbi' into their shul, as the 'driver' — who was the actual rabbi — walked close behind. Once in the shul, they wined and dined him, while the 'driver' sat in the back.

Then, the scholars of the village sat down with the 'rabbi' and asked, "We have a very difficult question on the law that none of us can interpret. We've been waiting months until you'd come to solve it for us." They then placed a huge book before the 'rabbi,' who could not even read Hebrew.

He studied the page dramatically for a few minutes, then turned to the scholars, "My friends, this is so simple, even my driver could answer this!"

With that, he turned to the real rabbi, dressed as the driver, handed the book to him and exclaimed, "Will you please explain this passage to these people!"

I n some shuls, they auction off the honor of reading a portion of the Torah during the High Holiday services.

As the holidays approached, Goldberg invited his partner, who was an Irishman, to spend the holidays with his family. As Goldberg prepared to go to shul, his Irish partner asked. "Could I go along to see one of your services?" Goldberg was flattered, and the two went to shul.

For an hour, the Irishman sat spellbound, watching attentively as the solemn service unfolded. Finally, there came a lull and the selling of the ritual honor began.

"$20 for *maftir*" called out the gabbai.

"$30!" Goldberg called out proudly.

The Irishman looked at Goldberg then stood up and shouted, "I bid $60 dollars!"

Goldberg grabbed his partner's arm and whispered excitedly, "Have you lost your mind? You can't bid on this!"

The Irishman turned with a smile, "Listen, Goldberg, I've known you for 30 years. If you offer $30, why shouldn't I offer $60? It has to be worth at least $100!"

· ·

I t was back in the late 1800's when Horowitz came to our shores. To those in Europe it was America — the land of the free — where the streets were supposed to be paved with gold. In those years, who had streets? As a result of this sad awakening, Horowitz got a basket and began to sell needles and pins.

He worked day and night, but soon realized there had to be something better — after all he was in America!

One day, he learned that a shul needed a *shammes* to care for the building, so he applied for the job. When the president of the shul was interviewing him for the job, he was asked to write his name.

"I'm sorry," he said sadly, "But I never learned to write."

"What?" exclaimed the president of the shul, "You never learned to write? I'm sorry, in this job one has to know how to write. This is not the old country. This is America! Here, everyone has to learn to write to succeed." Horowitz was turned away and he went back to his peddling.

Over the years, he had saved enough to buy a small piece of real estate. Then another, and then another. In a few years, after some wheeling and dealing, he had real estate holdings worth more than $10 million dollars.

Now that Horowitz was a wealthy, charitable man, a local shul wanted to honor him. They hired out the main ballroom at the Waldorf Astoria hotel. Notables from all over the nation came to pay honor to this financial genius. Even the President of the United States sent official greetings.

At the dinner, the president of the shul sat with Horowitz and asked almost embarrassed, "Could you give me your autograph? It's for my grandchildren."

Horowitz smiled uneasily and made an "X." The president of the shul turned in amazement, "You mean to tell me you can't even sign your name? My goodness, how one person could accomplish so much without even being able to write!

Could anyone imagine what you would have been today had you been able to simply write your name?"

Horowitz smiled weakly and exclaimed, "Of course, I probably would have been the *shammes* of the shul!"

. . . .

It was Shavuot, and the rabbi's wife made up a batch of blintzes to be dropped off at a young doctor's house. When the rabbi got there, the doctor was out on call, so he decided to leave them in the milk box, which was near the front door. He figured they would stay warm since the box was insulated.

He left a note on the door, which read, "Have a happy holiday, the blintzes are in the milk box."

When the young doctor returned home, there was another note stuffed in the door. It was from the milkman and read, "Thanks a million for the blintzes, they were still warm. Really, how many people remember their milkman on Shavuot?"

. . . .

Little Irving accidentally swallowed a dime and his mother began to panic. She turned the child upside down, but try as she could, the money didn't come out.

"Quick — call the doctor!" she shouted to her husband.

"Doctor, nothing!" shouted the husband, "I'm gonna get Rabinowitz, the president of our shul! He can get money out of anybody!"

Once upon a time, a young man found a wallet with $100 in it. As he looked through the wallet, he discovered there was no identification and nothing that could determine who the owner was.

A few days later, the rabbi in the shul made an announcement that one of the wealthy members of the congregation had lost his wallet. The description the rabbi gave fit the description of the wallet that the young man found. The young man promptly went to the rich man's house and, after being let in, asked the rich man, "Is this the wallet you lost?"

The wealthy man grabbed the wallet and quickly pulled out the money. All the money was there. Then, thinking the young man would ask for a reward, he turned sharply and said, "Where is the other $100 that was in here? There were $200 in this wallet, now there is only $100! You better run before I call the police!" The young man ran away fearing the wrath of the wealthy man.

As he ran, he met the rabbi and explained to him what had happened. The rabbi went with the youth to the house of the wealthy man.

"Tell me, my friend," the rabbi exclaimed. "You said you lost a wallet that had $200 in it. This youth, who is an honorable man, swears there was only $100 in the wallet when he found it."

"So?" exclaimed the stingy man.

"So!" replied the rabbi, "Please return the wallet and the $100 that was in it to this young man, because by your own admittance your wallet contained $200, while this contained only $100. Obviously, this is not your wallet."

The rabbi took the wallet and the money, handed it to the youth and they both walked away, to the bewilderment of the wealthy man.

. . . .

One day, a non-Jewish peasant came to a rabbi and spoke haltingly. "Rabbi," I have heard so much about Talmud and it puzzles me. What is Talmud?"

The rabbi smiled and exclaimed, "Talmud, my friend, ahhh! It takes great knowledge to understand the Talmud. I doubt whether you have this knowledge."

"Please try to teach me," the fellow begged. "Try me, see if I can understand."

The rabbi smiled and said, "All right, we'll try. Now, if two burglars enter a house by the way of a chimney, and then find themselves in the living room of their victim, one with a dirty face and the other a clean face, which one would wash his face?"

The peasant thought for a moment, then said, "Why, the one with the dirty face, of course!"

"You see," said the rabbi, "You could not understand Talmud — the one with the clean face would look at the one with the dirty face and, assuming his own face was dirty, would wash it. Yet the one with the dirty face would look at the one with the clean face, and seeing that the other fellow's face was clean, would not wash his own face."

The peasant smiled knowingly and said, "Thank you Rabbi, thank you. Now I see the complexities of Talmud."

"No you don't," sighed the rabbi, "Who but a peasant would think that when two burglars enter a house by way of the chimney only one would have a dirty face?"

. . . .

One Shabbat morning, the rabbi noticed little David was staring up at the large plaque that hung in the foyer of the shul. It was covered with names, and small American flags were mounted on either side. The 7-year-old had been staring at the plaque for some time, so the rabbi walked over to him and said, "Good Shabbos, David."

"Good Shabbos," replied the youngster, still focused on the plaque. "Rabbi, what is this plaque about?" the youngster asked.

"Well, son, it's a memorial to all the young men and women who died in service."

Soberly, they stood together staring at the names. The child's voice was barely audible when he asked, "Rabbi, which one — the Friday night or the morning service?"

. . . .

Sam, Irving, and Louie were the cheapest guys in town. Whenever an appeal was made in the shul, the three of them always sat in the back and quietly slipped out. This time, the president of the shul decided he was going to get them and reserved for them three seats in the very front row.

The three of them came in and sat down. As the rabbi got

up to make the appeal, Sam pretended to faint, while Irving and Louie carried him out.

. . . .

Shloimy Yachenflaster, who was not a very well-liked landlord, had passed away. At his funeral, the rabbi said, "I cannot be critical of Mr. Yachenflaster, but I believe at least one of his tenants might say a kind word in his behalf."

One tenant stood up and the rabbi whispered to him, "Just say something nice about him in a few words."

The tenant took a deep breath and said, "Well, let me put it this way. His partner was worse than him!"

. . . .

The father of a young boy who was going to be Bar Mitzvah, spoke with his son. "My dear Sheldon, Mama and Papa love you very much, so we want to make your Bar Mitzvah something special. Would you like to have it in Russia where your great-grandparents lived? Or, would you like to have it Florida, where Mama's family lived? Or would you like to have it in Manhattan, at one of the big hotels?"

The kid thinks for a minute and says, "I would really like to have it in Japan."

The father and mother look at the youngster and say, "Japan? Why Japan?"

The kid sighs, "So if I make a mistake while reading from the Torah, who will know?"

The old rabbi was trying to teach his little group of youngsters an understanding of values.

"If I had a watch that ran fast all day long and I had another watch that did not run at all — which watch is of greater value?" the old man asked the youngsters.

One little one raised his hand and said, "I would keep the watch that ran fast — at least it runs."

"Wrong," exclaimed the rabbi. "Here is the essence of value. You should keep the watch that did not run at all — because the watch that ran fast would never give you an accurate time, but the watch that did not run at all, at least it would be correct twice a day!"

· ·

The rabbi approached Mrs. Rabinowitz, "You know, Mrs. Rabinowitz, I was a little disturbed over what your husband did this Shabbos when I was giving my sermon. He walked out right in the middle."

Mrs. Rabinowitz smiled uneasily and replied, "Don't aggravate yourself, rabbi, he always walks in his sleep."

· ·

The rabbi, in his Elul sermon, spoke to his congregation about forgiveness. After his *drasha*, he asked how many were willing to forgive all those who had wronged them.

About half held up their hands.

Not satisfied, he spoke another twenty minutes and repeated his question. This time, he received a response of about 80%.

Still unsatisfied, he spoke on good *middos* for another fifteen minutes and repeated his question.

The congregation, hungry for kiddush, all raised their hands — all except for an elderly man.

"Reb Yankel, are you not willing to forgive your enemies?"

"I don't have any."

"That is very unusual, Reb Yankel. How old are you?"

"98."

"Reb Yankel, please tell us how you came to live to be 98, and not have an enemy in the world?"

The elderly man said, "I outlived them all!"

. . . .

The scout troop was meeting at the Jewish Center. When the rabbi interviewed the youngsters, he jovially asked, "And who did a good deed today?"

Five little fellows raised their hands. "We did, Rabbi! Today, the five of us took a little old woman across the street!"

"It took five of you to take her across the street?" the rabbi questioned.

"Yup!" snapped the little ones, "She didn't wanna go!"

The town's old sage sat studying, his long white beard resting on his chest. Slowly, his eyes began to close, until he seemed to be fast asleep. Nearby sat his students. When they saw his eyes close, one whispered to the other, "What piety, just look at that man, the warmest and best person in the world."

Another student looked at the old man and said softly, "Indeed. And his charity — who can compare with him?

He gives with his full heart."

"And his temper," said another, "Has anyone ever seen him lose his temper? He is an angel!"

"What brilliance!" another whispered.

The students studied him for a moment as the old man opened one eye cautiously and said sharply, "And about my modesty...none of you say a word?"

· ·

The young rabbi walked to shul with one of the old timers from the congregation. "Excuse me, Mr. Cohen," exclaimed the young rabbi one morning, "Why do you sleep through my sermons?"

The old timer smiled warmly and replied, "Because I trust you!"

· ·

There's a classic story told about a very wealthy woman who had made considerable donations to the shul. But she was a mean person, very inconsiderate of the feelings of others, and she constantly made life miserable for the rabbi.

However, whenever she was to appear at a shul function for women, she would always order the rabbi to write her speeches. No matter what pearls the rabbi wrote, they never seemed to satisfy the negative woman. She always found some fault — either it was bad or too long or too Talmudic — she was always able to conjure up something negative to say.

Finally, the rabbi was offered a post at another shul in a fine area, a shul where he felt he would be appreciated. He notified the congregation that he was leaving. However, the wealthy woman had one more speech to make and demanded that the rabbi write that last speech.

The rabbi tried to beg off, but the wealthy woman threatened all kinds of mean things if the speech wasn't written. Finally, the rabbi wrote the speech and handed it to her, who stuffed it into her purse, snapping, "This is probably too darn long. I'll read it when I have time!"

The nasty woman did not even review the speech. When the big annual woman's tea was taking place, she got up to make her speech. She pulled it out of her purse and read it in a matter of fact fashion.

Then she came toward the closing — which was marked with emphasis — she read out loud, "And I have solved the problem on how to stop anti-Semitism in this country. I have evolved ten methods that are sure fire for us all to follow."

She turned the page, and on the last page, the rabbi had written, "Okay, big shot, now you're own your own!"

Two college students were discussing religion and philosophy. "A philosopher is like a blind man in a totally dark room, looking for a black cat that isn't there," the student exclaimed.

"That may be," said the theology student, "But a rabbi would have found it!"

. . . .

Yankel was trying to observe the fast on Yom Kippur. But as the day wore on, hunger kept gnawing at him. Finally, in desperation, he slipped out a side door of the shul and went to a small restaurant nearby. The waiter walked over to him and said, "Yes?"

"Excuse me," he asked, "How much is a cheese sandwich?"

At that moment, there was deafening thunder-clap and a tremendous thunder storm erupted, shaking the building.

Frightened out of his wits, Yankel raised his eyes and his arms toward the heavens and shouted, "Listen, I was only asking!"

Travel

. . . .

A caddie goes over to a fellow playing golf and says, "Mister, I got this great little golf ball. You can't lose it." The golfer says, "Okay, but what happens if I hit it into the lake?"

The caddie says, "It floats. You can't lose it."

The golfer says, "What happens if I hit it into the rough?"

The caddie says, "It beeps. I'm telling you, you can't lose it!"

The golfer says, "And what happens if I play at night?"

The caddie says, "It glows. You can't lose it!"

The golfer says, "That sounds great. Where did you get it?"

The caddie says, "I found it!"

A fellow was riding along the New York Thruway at the proper speed, when suddenly, he was flagged down by a motorcycle cop.

"Pull over!" shouted the officer,

"What's the trouble?" the man questioned, "I wasn't speeding!"

"I know you weren't speeding," replied the officer, "But your tail lights are both out, so I have to give you a ticket."

"Oh my!" shouted the man. "Oh my! Oh, this is terrible!" he continued shouting while running around the car frantically.

"Now, wait a minute," consoled the cop, "I have to give you a ticket, but it's not so terrible! It's only a $5 fine. What's the big deal?"

The man continued moaning, "Sure, to you it's only a small fine, but to me it's a wife and three children and a trailer. Heaven knows how far back they were disconnected from the car!"

A little old lady from Brooklyn was taking her first airplane ride. As she boarded the plane, she held a copy of a Jewish newspaper in her hand. She was seated next to a man who noticed the paper and sneered, "Hmmm, just my luck to sit next to a Jew!"

The little old lady did not say a word. As the plane got ready for the takeoff, the anti-Semite began to carry on about sitting next to a Jew.

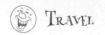

When the stewardess came around, he ordered a few hefty whiskeys, then settled back in his seat and fell promptly asleep.

As the plane reached cruising altitude, it hit a series of air pockets. The little old woman became ill and accidentally threw up on the anti-Semite sitting next to her.

Soon, the anti-Semite awoke and looked at the mess all over his jacket and then, menacingly, at the old lady.

She smiled pleasantly and asked, "Are you feeling better?"

. . . .

A man entered a hotel in a suburban community and was told that the charges were $5 a day for rooms on the first floor, $4 for rooms on the second floor, $3 for rooms on the third, and $2 on the top floor. After a minute of reflection, he started for the door when the clerk asked him if he considered the charges too high.

"No," he replied, "It's the building that's not high enough!"

. . . .

A rabbi traveling through Georgia got off his bus by mistake in a small town. He walked through the village and then approached a heavy-set fellow sitting in a rocking chair.

"Excuse me," said the rabbi, "Could you tell me where the synagogue is in this town?"

The southern bigot turned nastily and said, "We don't allow Jews in this village."

The rabbi smiled uneasily and replied as he walked away, "That's probably why it's still a village!"

. . . .

A stingy old timer was having a bell-hop pick up his bags from his room to take to the curb before he departed for home. The bell-hop smiled with his hand out, "I hope you won't forget me..."

The old timer smiled back, "Of course not. I'll write the minute I get home!"

. . . .

A sweet little old lady was taking her first airplane ride and was a little frightened. The stewardess noticed her fear and said, "Here's a few things to keep you occupied," and she handed her a magazine. "Oh, and if your ears bother you," the stewardess continued, "Here's a few pieces of gum."

The little old lady thanked the stewardess and enjoyed a pleasant, but uneventful, flight. As she prepared to get off and passed by the stewardess, she exclaimed, "That gum worked wonders, but please tell me, how do I get it out of my ears?"

. . . .

A woman wrote to a fancy resort hotel to find out if they allowed pets at the hotel. She was considering going to that hotel and was very attached to her pet.

The manager of the hotel, who was also a pet-lover, wrote

back, "Dear Madam, I have been in the hotel business for some 28 years. Never in all that time have I had to call the police to reject a disorderly pet at 4:00 AM. Never once has a pet set fire to a room by carelessly dropping a lighted cigarette. Never has a pet stolen any of my towels, bedspreads, or even silverware. Of course your pet is welcome at the hotel"

It was signed, "Sincerely, the Manager."

At the bottom of the letter was a P.S., "If the pet will vouch for you, you can come too!"

. . . .

A young family went to the Catskills for vacation. When they arrived at a hotel, the father stepped forward and asked the clerk, "Excuse me — how much do you charge for a room?"

The hotel clerk declared, "Well, we have two types, one is $10 a room and the other is only $2 a room."

"What's the difference between the $2 room and the $10 room?" the man asked.

"Well, with the $10 room, we make your beds. In the $2 room, you have to make your own beds," the clerk explained.

"Oh, that's all right," exclaimed the mother." We can take the $2 room."

"Fine," exclaimed the desk clerk. "You'll find the wood in the basement and a hammer and nails in the closet!"

A youngster who was flying from California, kept running up to the airplane attendants and asked, "Where are we now? What city are we flying over now?"

The attendants would stop what they were doing, refer to the flight schedule, and explain to the youth where they were.

This went on every twenty minutes. Finally, an attendant said, "Here, let me give you the flight schedule and all you have to do is look at your watch and from the time elapsed between places, you will be able to tell where we are."

This apparently satisfied the youngster for about an hour. Then he ran up to the attendant once more and asked, "Where are we now?"

The attendant turned and said, "Why don't you look at your watch?"

The kid replied, "Because somebody stole my watch a few minutes ago."

The hostess smiled warmly, "Oh, then we are over New York!"

. . . .

An elderly Jewish couple on their way to a vacation in Hawaii got into an argument about the correct pronunciation of "Hawaii." He was sure it was "Havaii" but she maintained it was "Hawaii."

As soon as they landed, they asked the first person they saw, "Would you mind telling me the name of this island?"

"Havaii!" replied the man.

"Thanks," answered the man.

"You're velcome!" said the man.

. . . .

An old timer was coming to America aboard an old cargo ship. Suddenly, a storm came up and the ship started to list to one side. The old timer just stayed near the railing, looking at the sea.

Just then, the captain passed by and said, "Gee, you're wonderful. Everyone is panicking. Aren't you even concerned about this ship crashing into the rocks or simply sinking at sea?"

The old timer shrugged, "Why should I worry? Do I own the ship?"

. . . .

Cohen and his wife were in Europe. When they went to the famous art museum, The Louvre, in Paris, and saw the original painting of the 'Mona Lisa,' Mr. Cohen sighed, "Isn't that beautiful?"

Mrs. Cohen was not impressed. She replied, "What's the big deal? We have the same picture on our calendar in the kitchen!"

Goldberg and Lapidus were partners for many years in the Garment Center. One year, Goldberg took a trip to Europe to look over styles for the new fall line. As he left one style house, a Frenchman sidled up to him and asked, "Monsieur, would you like to purchase an original Rembrandt, a Rembrandt that is so famous, the French government would not permit it to be shipped out of France?"

Goldberg asked, "So how would you get it out of France if I should want to buy it?"

"Leave that to me," exclaimed the Frenchman who then took Goldberg to his studio. There he revealed the great painting.

"And it's only $500,000 — it is worth three times as much once you have it in America!" the Frenchman exclaimed.

Goldberg was fascinated and gave the Frenchman a check. "Now tell me," asked Goldberg, "How will you get it to America for me?"

"Simple," the Frenchman exclaimed, "My partner, Garachi, will paint a picture over the Rembrandt and the French authorities will think the painting is a cheap Garachi and let it go through customs. When you get it to America, all you have to do is wipe off the Garachi and voila, you have the Rembrandt."

Goldberg was thrilled. When Garachi had finished painting over the Rembrandt, it was quickly crated and sent to the dress house of Goldberg and Lapidus in New York City. Goldberg was thrilled. He could hardly wait to hear from his partner.

Finally, a cablegram arrived. It was from Lapidus. He cabled, "Received the Garachi and did like you said, cleaned

off the paint. Found Rembrandt. I cleaned off the Rembrandt. Found another Garachi. How far should I go?"

. . . .

Goldberg decided to go to Las Vegas for his vacation. No sooner had his plane landed than he found himself sitting at a roulette table. With every spin of the wheel, he lost more and more. Finally, all he had left was a single chip. He closed his eyes in silent meditation and suddenly he heard an unearthly whisper, which said, "Play 18 — *Chai!*"

He fingered the chip nervously and placed it on number 18. Sure enough, the little ball stopped rolling and settled on number 18. Just as he started to reach for his winnings, he heard that heavenly voice again, "Let it ride, Goldberg...let it ride..."

He let the chips ride on number 18, and sure enough, when the little ball stopped rolling, it settled on number 18 again. He had won close to $3,000.

Just as he reached for the chips, he heard the heavenly voice whisper again, "Goldberg, don't be a fool, let it ride — 18 is your lucky number...let it ride!"

So Goldberg let it ride once more.

The wheel spun and, sure enough, the little ball stopped rolling and landed on the number zero.

He lost everything.

As he looked up and waited for guidance from that heavenly voice, he heard, "Don't complain, you only lost one chip!"

Goldberg boarded a plane with a tiny Yorkshire Terrier on a leash. He sat down in his seat with the dog next to him. In a few minutes, the stewardess walked over to him and said, "I'm sorry sir, but you are not allowed to have a dog on this plane."

Goldberg, wearing dark glasses asked, "Doesn't the law say that seeing-eye dogs are permitted on planes?"

The stewardess said, "Why, yes."

"Well, I'm blind and this is my seeing-eye dog," he replied.

"That's different," the stewardess replied. "But I thought all seeing-eye dogs were German Shepherds," she said.

Goldberg clutched his heart and screeched, "*Gevald!* You mean he's not?"

. . . .

I can't understand why people worry so much about their vacations; they are actually so easy to plan: The boss tells you when and your wife tells you where.

. . . .

In deepest Africa, a group of tourists are being taken through the jungle. Suddenly, they hear the sound of a native drum banging away. As they come closer to the village, they see a witch-doctor pounding away on the drum.

One of the tourists goes over to the witch doctor and asks, "Why are you beating the drum?"

The witch doctor says, "We have no water."

The tourist nods his head as if he understands, then says, "So you're calling on the rain spirits to bring you water?"

The witch doctor smiles courteously and says, "No, I'm sending for the plumber!"

. . . .

Moe could not write a word of English, nor could he even sign his name. Whenever he had to sign his name, he would merely dab his thumb into the inkwell and leave a thumb-print impression. Most of his business associates understood, and the places he traveled to always accepted this as his signature.

After traveling a whole day, Moe and his partner arrived at a hotel for the night. He walked up to the clerk and was handed a pen to sign in. Moe promptly dipped his pinky in his little inkwell and left the pinky print on the spot where he was to sign.

His partner looked at him strangely. "All the time you sign your name by leaving a thumb-print, so how come now you make a mark with your pinky?"

Moe smiled slyly and whispered, "Shhh...I didn't want to leave my real name!"

One special mountain resort prided itself on an exercise program they had for their clients. Each vacationer was to perform a certain number of exercises each morning. However, one guest flatly refused. He said indignantly, "I came for rest, relaxation, and food — not to exercise!"

When it came time for the guest to check out, the owner met him at the check-out desk.

"Mr. Goldberg, I want to thank you for being our guest — but, could you do me one favor?"

The guest replied, "*Nu*, ask!"

"I wonder," began the hotel owner, "If you could just do a simple exercise for me. You see, in our advertisements we say every guest exercises. Even just a bit of exercise is all you have to do so I shouldn't be called a liar."

"*Nu*, so what do you want me to do?" questioned Goldberg.

"Please," began the owner, "See if you can pick up your suitcase over there near the door and carry it over to this desk. Such a simple exercise is all I request."

Goldberg grudgingly went over and picked up the suitcase and brought it over to the hotel owner.

"Now, one more thing," asked the owner, "Could you bend down low enough and touch your suitcase?"

The guest did a deep knee bend and touched the suitcase grudgingly. "*Nu* — now what?"

"Now," shouted the hotel owner, "Open the suitcase, and give back my towels!"

Sadie and Sam were in a hotel on their vacation, when suddenly somebody shouted, "Fire! Fire! Fire! All the stairways are on fire!" Sam shouted to his wife, "Quick, quick, let's jump out the window!"

Sadie turned and screamed, "What? We're on the 13th floor!"

Sam put his hands on his hips and hissed, "All of a sudden you're superstitious?"

. . . .

Sadie and Sam were married forty years and were touring the mountains of Israel. When they got out to tour, Sadie said to Sam, "You know, I hope this mountain air doesn't disagree with me."

Sam sighed, "Darling, it wouldn't dare!"

. . . .

Sadie and Sam were on a ship, when it broke apart and they found themselves in the middle of the ocean, hanging on to a raft for dear life.

Suddenly, Sadie, seeing a sailboat on the horizon, shouted excitedly, "Sam, a sail...a sail...!"

Sam shouted back, "We're drowning, and she wants to go shopping!"

Sadie decided to take her mother for a trip through the Rocky Mountains to show her real Americana. As they passed one of the more scenic areas, Sadie commented, "Ma, look at that view. Isn't it beautiful?"

The old lady sighed, "What view? The mountains are always in the way!"

. . . .

Sadie had just returned from Europe. When she met with the girls from the sisterhood, they asked her, "Dahlink, when you were in Europe, did you pick up any Picassos or Van Goghs?"

Sadie smiled knowingly, "Of course not — we didn't drink the water."

. . . .

Sam and Ida went to a very expensive resort in the mountains. In the evening, they noticed some of the help who worked in the kitchen walking on the grounds.

"Sam," Ida exclaimed, "Look how nicely the dishwasher is dressed."

Sam shrugged, "And why not? He was probably a guest here a week ago!"

Selma Epstein made her very first trip to Paris and decided to go on a shopping spree. She ran to one shop after another, then stopped at one little shop where they sold tablecloths.

"*Bon jour, mademoiselle,*" began the salesgirl.

Selma smiled warmly and showed the tablecloth to the saleslady and asked, "*Madame, combien coûte cette tishtach?*"

The salesgirl smiled knowingly and replied, "*Mille francs pour cette tishtach.*"

"*C'est un shmattah!*" snapped Selma.

"*Mademoiselle,*" began the saleslady, "*Ce n'est pas shmattah, c'est un grand metziah!*"

Selma became angry and snapped, "*J'ai dit un shmattah, et un shmattah!*" and she stormed out of the shop.

The salesgirl turned to the store manager and, shaking her head in disgust, explained, "*Ces Américains — quelle chutzpah!*"

. . . .

The huge bus in a Georgia bus station pulled to a halt. A burly Southerner got on the bus and spotted a yeshiva boy. He walked over to his seat and noticed a package next to him.

"Get that package off that seat!" ordered the bully.

The yeshiva bochur just sat motionless and did not say a word to him.

"Oh, a wise guy!" shouted the bigot, "I said, take that package off that seat!"

The yeshiva boy remained motionless and silent.

"Now you're trying my patience!" shouted the bigot, as he leaned over, picked up the package and threw it out the window.

"Now," he roared, "That ought to teach you a lesson!"

The yeshiva boy smiled meekly, "Why should it teach me anything? The package belongs to the bus driver. Now watch what he's going to do to you!"

. . . .

Two old timers were talking. "I went to Atlantic City for some change and some rest."

His friend asked, "*Nu*, so did you accomplish what you went for?"

The friend replied, "Not really. The bellboy got the change and the hotel got the rest!"

. . . .

Two women were discussing their summer vacations. "*Nu*, Sophie, so where did you go this summer for your husband's vacation?"

"We went to Aruba," Sophie replied.

"How exciting! And where is Aruba?" the first women asked.

"*Ver vais?*" Sophie replied unconcerned, "We flew!"

 TRAVEL

Two young men in a mountain resort were having a cultural discussion. "Say, Irving," the first fellow asked, "Do you know the difference between valor and discretion?"

Irving replied, "Well, an example of valor would be staying at this hotel for a week then leaving without tipping the waiter."

"And what would be discretion?" the friend asked.

Irving replied. "Not coming back here again!"